Foreword by Dr. Larry Osborne

Circles Not Rows

The Power of Small Groups and Strategy that Works

Circles Not Rows

The Power of Small Groups and Strategy that Works

Dave Enns

All Rights Reserved. No portion of this book may be reproduced, stored in a retrieval system, or transmitted in any form or by any means -- electronic, mechanical, photocopy, recording, scanning, or other -- except for brief quotations in critical reviews or articles without the prior permission of the author.

Published by Game Changer Publishing

Paperback ISBN: 978-1-962656-11-5
Hardcover ISBN: 978-1-962656-12-2
Digital: ISBN: 978-1-962656-13-9

www.GameChangerPublishing.com

DEDICATION

To the pastors, leaders, and people who believe in the power of connecting in circles and not just rows. I hope this helps you keep the main thing the main thing

- loving Jesus and others!

DOWNLOAD YOUR FREE GIFTS

Read This First

Just to say thanks for buying and reading this book, we would like to give you a few free bonus resources, no strings attached!

Scan this QR Code:

Forward by Dr. Larry Osborne

Church happens in …

Circles Not Rows
The Power of Small Groups and Strategy that Works

Dave Enns

www.GameChangerPublishing.com

Acknowledgments

Many thanks to …

My friend group in high school. Stan, Jeff, Todd, and Jeff. What happened with us back then still stands today, giving me confidence that friends following Jesus makes a difference.

Larry Osborne, my boss and mentor. This book is your heartbeat for the local church, not just North Coast. You laid the foundation for our small groups at North Coast, and your vision and persistence ensured they were always of the highest priority. Your leadership and wisdom have guided me not only in ministry but also in showing me how to love my family first, work hard, and then take a nap.

Chris Brown, my leader and friend. You have helped North Coast reach more than we could have imagined while still holding groups and relationships as our unwavering measure of health. I know no one who works harder while embodying the enthusiasm and hope that our God gives us. Your consistent encouragement motivates me to grow and use my God-given gifts and abilities. I could not be more thankful for your commitment to helping make this book happen.

Charlie Bradshaw, my former boss, continuing mentor, and friend for over two decades. I would not be where I am today without you. Your belief in me (and most everyone) never stops. I can always rest in it. So many of us are better because of you. My hope is to do for others what you have done for me.

Ned Mervich, my ministry partner, colleague, and friend for the past seventeen years! This book is essentially ours, having taught this content with you for the past decade. Your feedback on points to highlight as I wrote has been essential. Your friendship, encouragement, and thought-provoking questions are what I cherish the most.

The North Coast Life Group team and the entire North Coast Staff. The content of this book is ours, not mine. As a team, you embody the power of a circle. This doesn't happen just because of the Life Group team, but because our entire staff is committed to it. Your persistence in keeping North Coast about relationships with Jesus and others and your full commitment to having fun along the way is working! It's never a dull moment coming to work and knowing that your love for Jesus and others is your highest priority.

All of you who were in Life Groups with my wife, Koreena, and I over the past 33 years. You have allowed me to take off my pastor hat and be unapologetically myself. You have been a place to connect, refocus, laugh with, cry with, and do life with. You are our lifelong friends. You help make following Jesus real and hopeful. You are the fabric of what makes the contents of this book true. I wish I could spend more time with all of you.

To my closest friends who walk beside me, you have grown me and pushed me. You know me better than I realize. You have seen all my sides, and yet you remain. Thank you for your grace. Your presence motivates me, and your encouragement has helped push me beyond my own doubts.

My prayer warriors. The 34 of you who have prayed weekly for me over the time it took to write this book, I never quite understand how prayer works, but I know it does. Your prayers have been effective and helpful.

The many who encouraged me to put these ideas into words and who gave me the time and space to process and refine my ideas verbally. Chris Surrat and Steve Gladen, five years ago, you said, "Get what you do into words!" Thank you for your consistent belief in my ability to share life-changing principles.

To the many who spoke into this book and made suggestions to make it better. A special thanks to Trent Jenkins and Philip Byers, my friends and coworkers who always spoke to the positive, helped trim the excess and kept me affirmed. Koreena and Kassidy, your availability and insight on rewriting to expand upon an idea go unmatched. And Vikki Almond, I am so thankful your ability to read my mind has grown even more! This day would not be here without you bringing clarity, forward momentum, and laughter when it was needed the most. Thank you.

Alex, my publisher from Gamechanger, you were always ready to engage. You kept me focused and motivated.

Mom and Dad, for your unconditional love for me and all of us kids, our spouses, and your grandkids. There has never been a question of how much you love all of us, Jesus, and anyone around you in need. People have always been what matters most to you, and I thank you for modeling and instilling those values in me since childhood.

To my family: Koreena, Kassidy, Sean, Landen, Jenna, and Sabrina. You are the joy of my life. Your love for Jesus, affirmations, laughter, ideas, can-do attitudes, and real questions about life and faith fill me and many others up beyond what you know. Koreena, my fellow adventurer for 32 years! You are the love of my life. I thank God over and over again for the wisdom you offer to me and our kids. The sounding board you provide for my many words is a cherished space, and you have always made our home a place of rest and comfort in the midst of the crazy space of writing. Your help through this process goes beyond what I could fathom, and your patience embodies Christ's love. I'm excited about what God has in store for us next!

Endorsements

"Dave Enns has been a model for the connected life for many years, personally with those who know him best and organizationally through his leadership at North Coast Church. Dave is authentic, insightful, and helpful. He has been immensely effective at prioritizing what matters most, which is people's lives with God as evidenced by their life with a few others. I am so excited for us that Dave finally took the time to write down many of his personal and leadership insights in Circles Not Rows. It is so worth the wait and so worth the read. Your church and small group ministry will be the better for it. And so will you."

> Bill Willits
> Executive Director – Ministry Environments
> North Point Ministries • Alpharetta, Georgia
> Co-author, Creating Community: *Five Keys to Building a Thriving Small Group Culture*

* * *

"This is the small group book I have been waiting for! North Coast Church is a pioneer in many facets of ministry - particularly small groups. We finally have the inside scoop! Whether you are looking to reforge your groups from the ground up, start fresh, or tweak your ministry, you will underline, dog ear, and highlight this book. Full of wisdom, Dave shares his experience and North Coast's proven system. Every small group pastor needs to buy - and read - this book!"

> Bill Search
> Executive Pastor at Crossings Community Church
> Author of Essential Guide for Small Group Leaders

"I so wish I would have had this book 15 years ago! I have leaned on North Coast and Dave's wisdom on groups for many years, and now I am so happy that it is in a book for every leader to learn from. These aren't theoretical discipleship ideas, but time-tested strategies that will produce fruit in your groups' ministry."

>   Chris Surratt
>   Author of Small Groups for the Rest of Us and Leading Small Groups
>   Executive Pastor of Discipleship and Groups, Harvest Christian Fellowship

* * *

"No matter what the size of your church, this is a must-read if you want the best possible small group ministry. Dave provides practical principles, best practices, processes, resources, and a philosophy for creating healthy and thriving small groups."

>   Dr. Charlie Bradshaw, Executive Pastor -North Coast Church (retired)
>   Author, Too Hurried to Love

* * *

"Dave's expertise in groups ministry is matched by his deep and genuine care for people. The wisdom and encouragement in these pages will be both foundational and motivational for anyone involved in ministry with groups. Dave brings depth, clarity and simplicity to a ministry that can easily get overly complicated and messy."

>   Natalie Myers
>   New Heights Church
>   Groups Director

"Dave's real-world experience, combined with practical knowledge, can help any small group point person looking to grow a healthy groups ministry. The strategies discussed in this book have helped our team grow and sustain a healthy small group ministry for decades at North Coast Church."

> Philip Byers
> North Coast Church
> Executive Pastor of Ministries

* * *

"North Coast and Dave Enns completely changed the way I viewed small groups in church. Learning and implementing this strategy has transformed the three churches I have had the privilege of serving in the last 10 years. In 25 years of ministry, nothing has produced this much life transformation and connection in our churches. Dave's wisdom, leading and willingness to share has impacted so many people he has never even met. This is a must read for all churches."

> Erin Rathier
> Groups Pastor
> Pure Heart Church

Foreword

The defining characteristic of the early church was community, not crowds. Unfortunately, too often today, we judge our churches by the size of the crowd, not the presence of community.

Yes, the early church experienced some amazing large group gatherings where thousands stepped over the line to follow Jesus. But the real power of the first century church wasn't found in what happened in those rare and powerful large gatherings. It was found in the homes, where the early believers gathered to support, encourage, challenge, pray, and teach one another.

The New Testament contains over thirty "one-another" commands. Few of them will ever take place in a large group of strangers (or mere acquaintances). It takes time, trust, and genuine relationships before we feel safe enough to share our real struggles, confront, pray, bear with, and forgive one another.

And to my thinking, that's one of the major weaknesses of our modern church. We've become experts at drawing crowds. But we are not so good at making disciples.

It's not for lack of effort. We talk, strategize, and pour lots of time, money, and energy into our "discipleship" ministries. But the results seldom match the effort.

Why? The problem is not our commitment. It's the context. We keep trying to make disciples in large group settings that work well when it comes to motivating, evangelizing, and passing along information, but not so well when it comes to fostering genuine life change. And many of our people think that spiritual maturity is evidenced by a growing one-on-one "personal" and intimate relationship with our Lord.

But our emphasis on large group settings and highly individualized concepts of spiritual maturity unintentionally leave out the most important tools (outside of the work of the Holy Spirit) for genuine discipleship: *The iron-sharpening-iron, godly peer pressure, advice, support, and prayer that happens in a group small enough that everyone actually knows and cares for one another.*

Long ago, when North Coast was about to break through the 200-attendance barrier, it hit me that those of us who had been here at the beginning were relationally connected and living out the one another's of scripture, and we were thrilled to add new acquaintances; but had no capacity to actually connect with any more people. So we were friendly. But we didn't connect.

Unfortunately, all the new folks that God was bringing to himself and our church weren't looking for a "friendly church." They were looking for friends!

That's when I decided that we would make Life Groups the hub of our ministry, using a lecture-lab model where the curriculum is sermon-based, and the focus is on relationships.

For nearly forty years now, that model has worked marvelously, producing disciples, assimilating new believers, and providing a place for the one-anothers of scripture to actually take place.

It's worked despite significant changes in culture and demographics. It's scaled from when we were a small church to the massive giga-church with multiple campuses that we are today.

For the past 20 years, Dave Enns has led the team that has successfully navigated the increasing complexity that has come with growth and the changing cultural and spiritual changes that have come with a changing calendar. And they've done far more than just maintain the successful ministry they inherited. They've significantly enlarged it.

In the following pages, Dave shares the principles, values, and strategies that he and his team have implemented over the years. We here at North Coast are incredibly grateful for the impact that Dave and his team have had upon North Coast. And I know you will be equally thankful for the impact that this book will have upon you and your small groups ministry.

Dr. Larry Osborne
North Coast Church

Table of Contents

Acknowledgments .... *ix*

Endorsements .... *xiii*

Foreword .... *xvii*

Introduction – My Story 1

Chapter 1 – Church Happens in Circles Not Rows 5

Chapter 2 – Purpose Matters 15

Chapter 3 – Ask Someone 29

Chapter 4 – Equip Someone 49

Chapter 5 – Connect Someone 73

Chapter 6 – Support Someone 89

Chapter 7 – Observe Someone Monitoring Your Results 107

Chapter 8 – Developing a Game Plan 117

INTRODUCTION

My Story

It was the summer before my junior year of high school when my buddies and I headed up to the rugged Sierra Nevada mountains for summer camp. As teenagers driving, taking on those windy, mountain roads, none of us anticipated that this summer would define us. There was plenty of rabble-rousing and antics, just as we expected. But what we didn't expect could not have been more timely. There were things we had to set right– mistakes acknowledged, forgiveness sought, and fresh paths chosen, not just as individuals, but as friends. It was a pivotal time for us. On that mountain top, the Holy Spirit was stirring in each of us personally and all the while creating a spiritual bond within our circle of friends. The challenges of teenage years had hit us hard yet this renewed purpose gave us strength we didn't realize. Strength laid upon the love, grace, and forgiveness that Jesus offers us. There was something about struggling together with our faith and humanity that anchored us. Still, it became evident that it wasn't just our faith keeping us rooted; our unyielding bond strengthened our faith.

Had you asked me back then, driving back from that life-changing trip, I'd have bet on the fact that those guys and I were in it for the long haul. Fortunately, time has proved that to be true. We no longer live close to each other, but we still talk and get together. Sometimes more, sometimes less, but never as much as we'd like. Life has taken us all to new places, with new hardships and new joys. Yet the power of that circle of friends remains, even to this day. Friends and faith. Little did I know then that creating these kinds of relationships and helping others do the same would essentially become my career and life's work.

We aren't designed to do life on our own.

At North Coast Church, friendship is important to us. It's one of the key measures used to assess the spiritual health of our church. For the past 20 years, I've helped people find their circle of friends through what we call Life Groups. In this position, I have had the opportunity to lead countless groups myself, recruited more leaders and hosts than I can remember, and trained thousands to join the team to help make it happen. It is the joy of my life.

Years ago, Larry Osborne, our founding pastor at North Coast Church and who I will refer to in this book as simply "Larry," made it his primary goal to enroll 80 percent of our adult weekend attendance in groups. The philosophy behind this was similar to what I experienced with my friends following that pivotal summer—that people in the church need to not only build a relationship with Jesus but also with each other. If you attend or listen to even just a handful of our services, it won't be long before you hear, "Church happens in circles, not in rows."

Since that time, I have continued to be baffled by the outcomes. Throughout our history, we've had 80 percent or more of adult weekend attendance involved in groups. For the past 12 years, more than 90 percent. Even when the COVID-19 pandemic hit in the Spring of 2020, nearly all our groups pivoted to virtual platforms. I was humbled to witness all that our leaders and hosts were willing to do so that they could continue to meet. It was especially during this time that I was convinced once again of how our church believes that relationships and following Jesus cannot be separated. It is working! Our people are building a lifeline of solid friendships centered on Jesus and his word.

In the following pages, I share key principles and practices we have learned along the way to help churches build a foundation for helping others create lifelong relationships with Jesus at the center.

CHAPTER 1

Church Happens in Circles Not Rows

"Show me your friends, and I'll show you your future."
- Anonymous

"Let us consider how we may spur one another on toward love and good deeds. Let us not give up meeting together as some are in the habit of doing, but let us encourage one another all the more as you see the day approaching." - Hebrews 10:24, 25.

It had been a year since we were on the team down on the field; now, we were in the stands watching. It was a high school football game and the team was on the five-yard line. The coach took too long to make the call, and a penalty was called, making it 10 yards to make the touchdown - twice as far as before! The people around us couldn't believe it. Their complaints were easy to hear. "He's not new at this coaching thing!" "He's calling plays like he's never been here before!" "Why would he take so long?" My friend next to me turned his head and looked at me with a grin. We knew exactly why. What people in the stands didn't understand is that it's much easier for the defensive player to guard the receiver if they only have five yards. But if it's 10 yards, the receiver has more room to make additional moves on the defensive player guarding him and is more likely to get open for the pass. And that's exactly what happened: a fast pass to the right side. TOUCHDOWN! What looked to be a blunder was genius. Great coaches can see what others don't and can maximize a team far beyond any individual talent.

Our coach won wherever he went, and not because he had the best players. In one of the seasons, this football team outscored their opponents with an average score of 49 to 1. Pretty amazing, isn't it? That was the year we played for them. It sounds like we had a bunch of superstars on our team, right? Wrong! We had only one player who made a D1 team during his college years. We also had only 18 active players for more than half the season. If you're not familiar with football, you need 11 players on each side of the ball to field a full team. That meant that through eight weeks of the season, we were never able to have a full team practice. He took a group of young guys who were passionate about a crazy sport like football and helped us do things we never thought we could because of the team, not the individuals. It was contagious, exhilarating and it took work! The result? Repeatedly overcoming opponents with far greater individual talent, but not nearly the team.

As pastors and leaders, we gravitate to a story like this. It reminds us of our calling and gives us hope and vision to help those we lead to see and experience the power of a group, as a team, as friends, and that it's not just about the individual! It's what we hope for in our church—the power of community, not just a crowd. It's contagious. It brings us in to be cared for and motivates us to go out to serve.

Yet, the enemy is keenly aware of the effect of community on spiritual health and growth, and therefore seeks to attack it. He knows how contagious and empowering it is! Because of this, he does everything he can to separate us from the vital life source of Christ-centered relationships. And he does so with deception, disguising his tactics, just like he did with Adam and Eve in the Garden of Eden, leading us to believe God's spirit is out of reach. This is why Paul warns us in 2 Corinthians 11:14 that Satan is "masquerading as an enemy of light." His trickery is masterful, his strategy diverse, and more often than we realize, it is built on deceptive half-truths of spiritual health. For this reason, it's vital we are able to recognize his three most destructive and yet subtle strategies he uses to thwart our faith and separate us from Christ:

#1 He wants to keep us stuck in sin and addiction. This is the one that easily gets our attention and that we likely preach and talk about the most. We focus on it because it's the most obvious. Our battle against sin is real, and the enemy is thrilled when we perpetuate patterns of sin in our lives. Sin either makes us despair that God's forgiveness and grace are out of reach, keeping us down, discouraged, and unmotivated, or it can grip us and lead us to believe that God is holding out on us. Sin and addiction can provide temporary pleasure and relief, putting our full focus on satisfying our own desires that continues to turn up our thirst for more. In the short term, we can feel good, even better, living in sin. It's appealing, otherwise we wouldn't do it. That's why it's so powerful and deceptive, keeping us stuck and blinded to true peace and joy.

#2 He wants to make our faith complicated. In Matthew 22:34-40, the Pharisees ask Jesus to name the most important commandment, a trick question intended to trap him in a longstanding, theologically complicated debate. Jesus sidesteps the question and deftly replies that the two essential components to obedient faith are "to love the Lord your God with all your heart, all your soul, and all your mind" and "to love your neighbor as yourself." Just like the Pharisees in this story, the enemy seeks to complicate our faith and create arbitrary barriers to entry into God's Kingdom. One way church leaders can unknowingly perpetuate this is in the way we talk to our members about Bible reading and study. The enemy wants people to believe if they only knew the Bible as well as their pastor (or any other spiritual mentor or person they look up to), they would have more of the Holy Spirit in their lives. People often mistakenly feel they would be more gifted and successful in their faith if they could quote biblical chapters and verses as their leader does. Nothing could be further from the truth.

Of course, Scripture is our guiding light and is vital to our relationship with Christ. It's the inspired word of God. I love how The Message states, "Every part of Scripture is God-breathed and useful one way or another—showing us the truth, exposing our rebellion, correcting our mistakes, training us to live God's way. Through the Word, we are put together and shaped up for the tasks God has for us" (2 Timothy 3:16-17). This is why we say we must all be committed to "being in the Word" and follow what it says. Yet, we must also be careful to not communicate that knowing the Biblical chapter and verse of all spiritual issues is the point of maturity and requirement for God's spirit to flow in our lives. Rather, we want our church to be committed to God and follow his Word in whatever way it may enter their hearts.

The ability to study and recall written text varies so greatly from person to person and is also a modern construct. We forget the Gutenberg Press wasn't productive until 1450. And that only 20% of the world was literate up until the 1900s. Reading your Bible even once was an impossible recipe for spiritual maturity for 80 percent of the world's population just a little more than 100 years ago. This is one of the reasons you will rarely hear pastors at North Coast tell our people to "read their Bible daily." Rather, we say, "Be in the Word regularly." It is a subtle, yet important difference. Being in the Word can take on many forms - not just reading but also listening, hearing teaching from others, group discussion, and conversations with friends. It's also why we create daily five-minute devotional videos for anyone to access throughout the week. We cannot miss Paul's important message of the "Priesthood of all believers" (2 Peter 2:9), which levels the playing field for all followers of Jesus, giving them equal access to our God and his spirit that works within us and helps us reach others for him.

#3 He wants to keep us isolated! The enemy wants you to think, *Jesus is all I need.* And he's right, theologically. But that's his trickery, taking something that's true and twisting it into a deception. He knows isolation tends to make our problems seem bigger than they are. We don't have access to support, encouragement, and accountability unless we have others around us. In isolation, we can fall into a downward spiral of spiritual deception that can sound like, "All you need is Jesus. So if you can't deal with this on your own, you're not depending on him enough." It can cause us to question why we're lacking if Jesus has given us all we need. Mistakenly, we can conclude, "I just need to pray more, read my Bible more, and do the right thing ... more! I need to be better!"

A person in this situation may benefit from prayer, Bible reading, and eliminating sin in their life, but they are missing a vital ingredient—engaging with an authentic community with Christ at the center. They are missing friends. Real friends with whom they can "bear one another's burdens" (Galatians 6:2). The enemy slips in the spiritual truth (only Jesus saves us) while smothering our understanding of spiritual health (we need Jesus and others)! If we gather regularly in an authentic community, we're going to encounter what we call "Holy Moments." Hebrews 10:24, 25 instructs, "Let us consider how we may spur one another on towards love and good deeds. Let us not give up meeting together as some are in the habit of doing, but let us encourage one another all the more as we see the day approaching." The enemy knows that when we gather, we will be encouraged, listened to, sped up, or slowed down, sharpened, hear God, help others, and get help—in essence, receive spiritual encouragement to be the best God has designed us to be. It's what we all need and desire. It's what God has designed to happen when we gather. What happens in groups is not designed by any church program or person - they are designed by God! These are Holy Moments. This is why the author of Hebrews tells Christians to not forsake meeting together. Doing so creates room for the enemy to gain a foothold to excuse sin, discourage us, and complicate the simple truths of living an abundant life with Christ. Consider the Garden of Eden—a perfect setting without sin. Despite its seeming perfection, God recognized it wasn't good for Adam because he was *alone*. Even Jesus, God incarnate, needed community. In the Garden of Gethsemane, Jesus, grappling with God about having to die for us, demonstrated his dependence on his disciples by asking them to pray with him. He did not intend to face this battle alone. Even Jesus called for the help of his community.

When I was a teen in church, I heard the verse "bad company corrupts good morals" (Corinthians 12:33) quoted to my friends and me quite a bit. I always thought this verse was directed at young people, instructing us about the importance of having good friends and not being around people who were a "bad influence." What I didn't realize is this verse was not written to youth—it was written to adults.

I remember when I was a junior high pastor, attending a parent meeting for an upcoming summer camp. I began to notice all the loveable quirks, strengths, and personality traits of my students reflected in their parents. I realized why the kids were the way they were. And that I was really in a room with a bunch of grown-up junior highers! Me included! If we're honest about how we live, we probably have more junior-high moments than we'd like to admit. Unfortunately, too often, we don't see that we can also digress to the darker side of junior attitude or response and be just as influenced by others as a junior higher would, but because we're "adults," we can think we can stand on our own and weather it. Our ability to be independent and self-sufficient are signs of mature adulthood, but also our kryptonite. Without authentic community and friends, we're not just alone—we're in trouble.

The groundbreaking 85-year study confirms it—life without friends increases heart disease by 32% and decreases longevity. It's equivalent to smoking 15 cigarettes a day! It included that these kinds of relationships take intentionality. They don't happen by accident. The latest study from the surgeon general states the United States is in the midst of an epidemic of isolation and loneliness. And this is after the COVID era of "forced isolation" has ended. We had an excuse then. But now? There's no question that there are concerns about how social media contributes to this. Yet, my concern is not the internet or social media—it's the local church. We have what people need. But are we offering it in a way that actually works?

Here's my question: at what level are we, as the church, taking this seriously? Or maybe a better question is, are we being intentional? I can't imagine any church not thinking seriously about the value of connection and relationships. But are we seriously doing anything about it… that's working? Or is the assumption among church leaders that relationships will "just happen" as a result of people attending a weekend service? No statistics are saying that's true.

As the church, we are in the business of helping our congregants build relationships with God and others. Yet, how much time, energy, and effective strategy are we really putting into that "others" piece? Returning to 1 Corinthians 15:33, when Paul says, "Bad company corrupts good morals," we should note that Paul addresses the Corinthians about the presence of people among them spreading false teachings about who Jesus is and questioning his resurrection. Isn't it interesting that Paul is refuting a theological problem by pointing out its relational roots? As I think about people I know who have fallen away from their faith in Jesus, most did not start with bad theology, but rather with a lack of or a negative relational influence.

Although it is not always the case that a person's fall from faith is from a lack of healthy Christ-centered people in their life, it's nevertheless important we do not underestimate the power of healthy relationships. The power and importance of holy moments that are created in community are crucial! It's not odd to hear that a church is committed to teaching the Bible. It's not uncommon to hear a church is committed to building relationships. Yet, in my experience working with churches, big and small, across the nation, many struggle to establish an intentional, effective strategy to connect the majority of their members to one another. I am concerned we're not paying attention to Satan's subtle attack to keep us isolated.

At North Coast, we believe that one of the most important discipleship decisions an individual can make is to join one of our small groups, which we call Life Groups. We want to do all we can to get them connected in vital relationships. When someone I know joins a Life Group at North Coast, I have a sense of relief. This is because I know they will most likely be in their Bible more than normal or ever do on their own. They'll be building friendships with people who will listen, laugh, and encourage them. They'll access other people's insights into what the Word says, which is especially important since, let's be real, most struggle with reading their Bible and studying on their own. They'll have a place to confess their sins, to get help when life is going hard, and be encouraged to live their life out for Jesus. They'll be up close and personal with those who are passionate about reaching and helping others follow Jesus, as well as with others who are struggling with their faith and trying to figure it out.

We're in an ever-changing landscape of culture. What church services have looked like over the decades, centuries, and millennials have changed immensely, and I'm sure they will continue to evolve. Yet, what has never changed is the power of a relationship with Jesus and others. The goal of the Church has never been about "me and Jesus," but rather about Jesus, me, and others so that we might live out a life with purpose, passion, and a grace-filled hope "To love God and Love others" (Matthew 22:37-40).

Let's assume that you are ready to dive into creating a bridge at your church to connect others in a relationship through healthy small groups. Or, quite possibly, you've recognized the importance but have not had the success you hoped for in creating or maintaining these groups. You may be wondering, *If we know that relationships are so important, why don't people join our groups? Why is it so hard to get leaders?*

If you're asking those questions, I'm glad you're here. In the following pages, I want to share with you our best practices and what has enabled us to maintain 80 percent or more of our adults involved in groups throughout our 37-year history of offering groups. This book is intended to be a scalable roadmap for those leading small group ministries.

One of the primary needs every person has when they walk through the doors of any church is to be connected in relationship—with God and others. That's why we do all we can to not only teach the Word but also to get our people connected with others. We don't see community as secondary to studying the Bible; the two are designed to go hand in hand. There is incredible power in a Christ-centered community (Hebrews 10:24, 25; John 13:35). Without it, the Christian is in a spiritual and relational deficit. It's one of the enemy's subtle strategies to keep followers of Jesus powerless and defeated. This is why our percentage in groups is so important to us.

I have no intent or desire for your church to become another North Coast. Similarly, when I discuss our benchmark of having 80 percent of our weekend attendance in groups, this doesn't mean you need to or should use this goal for your own church. Your church has its own significant DNA and unique part to play in the body of Christ. Rather, my hope is to offer you what we have learned over the years to help you affirm, build, and create spaces and circles where the people of your church and community can find friends to experience Holy Moments that will offer the life support they need to thrive, to follow Jesus, and help others to do the same.

We will do this by looking at six different areas of focus that have helped us succeed in our small groups. This is not a large or small church group model. It's a model we started almost 40 years ago when we were small and has continued to thrive through significant expansion. My hope is to help you build and create groups that will thrive over the long haul. So, let's go!

CHAPTER 2

Purpose Matters

"Good luck is another name for tenacity of purpose."
- Ralph Waldo Emerson

"Therefore, go and make disciples of all nations, baptizing them in the name of the Father, the Son, and the Holy Spirit, and teach them to obey everything I have commanded you, and surely I'm with you always to the very end of the age." - Matthew 28:19, 20

His energy was going to be good for the group. I'd seen it. We'd spent some time together at a number of men's events over the years. He was passionate about taking over leadership in one of our groups. He wanted to help and make an impact. The longtime hosts of the group were excited about him being their new leader and the enthusiasm he was going to add. The first meeting went well, as his new energy was good.

As the weeks progressed, I heard the transition with him was getting a little bumpy. Not surprisingly, that's part of new leaders entering in. It was a week later that I saw him with a smile on his face at one of our weekend services. "We did it," he proclaimed. "We had a great meeting last night."

Excited to hear about it, I asked what made it great. He said, "We finally answered every question."

I smiled and encouraged him, "I love that you're working hard at getting your group involved," and then mentioned, "Let's connect up this next week if we can and catch up a little."

I loved my friend's enthusiasm and hard work at leading, but his answer revealed quickly he wasn't clear on the purpose and strategy of what makes a great Life Group meeting. It also helped me understand why the leadership transition wasn't going well. His primary focus was getting through all the questions, not getting everyone involved. He was missing our purpose.

Our goal and purpose for our groups has never been to answer all the questions but rather to build friendships with Jesus at the center. Our strategy is to hear from everyone every time they meet. In fact, we clearly trained (so I thought) our new leaders that if you do hear from everyone, there's no way you'll answer all the questions.

He and I had a great meeting later that week. His heart was in the right place, and he did hear what our purpose was and how to accomplish it, but his enthusiasm and extroverted nature kept driving him to the wrong purpose of the meeting and missing the big-picture purpose of what was trying to be accomplished.

Clarity of purpose matters. It heads us in the right direction, maximizes our energy, and defines our success. Clarifying the purpose of your groups is essential for the same reason. My good friend Ned Mervich, a partner in ministry here at North Coast for seventeen years and team teacher of this content for a decade, illustrates how his understanding of groups evolved, affecting his expectation and intent of participation.

- The first is they are *informational*. It's a place where information is shared and discussed.
- Second, they are *inspirational*. The focus is to study together God's inspired word to us. You're not just discussing the information in it but being inspired by God's word through it.

- The third is *transformational*. It's not just about being inspired by God's word but building real friendships centered on Christ, creating the conduit for life transformation.

Every person who enters a group of any kind enters with a set of assumptions and expectations of what the group is about. It's what's going to drive them in the group and also how they will evaluate its success. The purpose you give your groups will do the same.

In the box below, in one sentence, write down why your groups exist. And if you don't have groups, write down why you think they should exist. Don't worry; you're not making any commitments. You're just putting your ideas down on paper. Take a minute to do this.

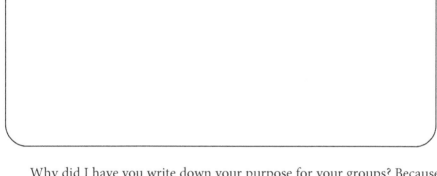

Why did I have you write down your purpose for your groups? Because your answer determines everything. It determines how you're going to train your leaders. It determines how and what you will be recruiting your leaders to lead. It's going to determine why your people are going to join your groups. It's going to determine how you evaluate whether your groups are successful and whether they are worth the time and effort that you are going to put into it.

Here are a few things to keep in mind as you think through how to determine the purpose of your small groups

Three Variables to Consider

#1 Understand and embrace your lead team or lead pastor's uniqueness, vision for your church, and purpose for your small groups.

We all want to make disciples and reach people for Jesus, and we all want to love God and love others. But we each have our unique ways of leading and making a difference. Dealing with these variances in focus and vision is important. Your lead team may see evangelism as an important element in your group. Maybe it's community service or deep theology.

One church I know is all about having an open seat for someone to join their group instantly. Another church is passionate about the process of discipleship development. And here at North Coast, we're all about just getting in a group—"You're going to grow on a need-to-know, need-to-grow basis as long as you keep God's word at the center." All three of these churches are reaching people for Jesus and helping them follow him. None are right or wrong. They're just different.

I've had small group pastors call me and share their frustration with their leadership team not catching the vision for groups and relationships within their church. It wasn't fitting what the group pastor saw as important. The frustration is understandable, and I, of all people, get it. Yet what's important, if you find yourself in this situation, is to focus on bringing new perspectives, options, and alternatives, and not just critique. God has brought your leader into your church for a reason. Be careful of degrading what God has called them to do. None of us want to become the focal point of creating division within the church.

The final chapter of this book helps you create a game plan to grow and/or launch your life groups. One of those keys will be defining your purpose for your groups. I've had teams that I've coached through this content, and after two days together, they knew their number one task when they returned home was to spend time clarifying their purpose rather than the overall implementation of a game plan. They actually had a great game plan, but they knew that without clarity of purpose, the motivation to create change and the ability to attain the resources needed would be a struggle.

#2 How does your church believe spiritual growth happens?

What would most people say? How about your staff? The usual answer I get is to read your Bible and pray and maybe go to church. And maybe share your faith. A less common answer is for someone to say that their relationships are vital to spiritual health or growth.

The mission at North Coast Church is to make disciples in a healthy church environment. We measure this in five ways in what we call the Five W's:

- Word - the practical teaching of God's Word.
- Worship - relevant participatory worship.
- Witness - seeing people come to know Jesus.
- Work - service involved in church and in the community.
- Warmth - the development of significant Christian relationships.

I'm guessing you picked up which one has to do with our groups: Warmth. Relational warmth, or friendship, is what our life groups are about—the development of those relationships is important because, as Larry set as our foundation long ago, that "we believe when you Velcro people to one another and God's Word, they will grow."

So often, growth is seen as just an individual or linear process. Yet, spiritual growth lived out is typically reflected through relationships. It is public, active, and not private (John 13:5; James 2:26; Matthew 22:37-39).

Genuine spiritual growth lived out offers real-life support to others and keeps God's Word at the center. And that's why we say we want 80% of our people involved in those relationships. The last thing we want to be is quiet in combating the enemy's subtle attack to keep us isolated. We want our people to be in circles where they encounter holy moments. To be encouraged and supported in those relationships. To create a lifeline friend that helps them hang on and follow Jesus.

Keeping our purpose in focus matters! Our purpose in groups is to develop significant Christian relationships. We do this by creating an environment where people can connect, create a safe place to deal with life and gain support, all based on the foundation of a commitment to follow Jesus with God's work in the middle. Everything we do, in all our leadership training and staff life group meetings, revolves around this central purpose. It's the signpost that keeps us heading in the right direction.

Create the Environment

We begin our new leaders and hosts training with this verse:

1 Corinthians 3:6-9, *"I planted the seeds. Apollo just watered it, but God has been making it grow. So neither the one who plants nor the one who waters is anything but only God who makes things grow. The one who plants, the one who waters has one purpose, and they will be rewarded according to their own labor. For we are coworkers and God serves it. You are God's field and God's building."*

When we read this to our new leaders, telling them they can't make anyone grow, we hear a "collective sigh of relief" in the room. Understandably, no one wants that kind of pressure. Of course, there's typically enthusiasm about taking on this new role in leading their group, but there's also the pressure to be responsible for making people grow! There's the enemy's trickery again, making us responsible for something that looks spiritually virtuous yet is impossible for us to do. It's here where we help our leaders redefine their role, guided by our purpose. Their role is to **create an environment** where people can connect, create a safe place to deal with life, and gain support, all based on the foundation of a commitment to follow Jesus.

One of the questions we ask the new leaders during the training is what makes a great life group meeting? The answers are diverse—a new biblical insight shared, vulnerability during a challenge in life, confession of sin, new wisdom, laughter, a new level of obedience, and of course, a great dessert is always mentioned. Those are all good answers. But do they make a great meeting? Well, they are great elements that show up one week and others the next week. Or perhaps these things are happening every meeting, but it's from the same people sharing each week. It can then negatively affect the group's primary purpose—for everyone in the group to build significant Christian relationships.

Why? Because what builds relationships, trust, encouragement, and a safe place to share is engagement with everyone, not hearing from the same few people every week.

Here's what we train our leaders to do and repeat to them over and over again that we believe makes a great meeting: Hearing from everyone every time you meet and keeping God's Word at the center. That's it. Could it be simpler? Here's why that's our philosophy: if you're not hearing from everyone every time you meet, it's like you're at a weekend service again, watching and listening, and NOT interacting with others again! It's so crucial, so simple, but so often missed. Again, the enemy loves to have people isolated, and if he can do it in a small group, it's an ultimate victory for him, leaving people to realize they're still alone, even in a small group.

Leaders often see it as their primary job to share wisdom and insight in scripture to help people follow Jesus. We hope at times, they can and will do that. Yet, their primary role is not to be the teacher or sage, but the facilitator.

In reality, their primary purpose is to help people build relationships, to become friends who listen to one another, and to encourage one another in life and as they follow Jesus. Our hope is that one of the key questions a leader will ask themselves after every time they meet is, did we hear from everyone? If so, it's a victory because they have taken on the role and significant task of helping to build relationships and facilitate an environment for growth.

#3 Can you measure your success?

How do you measure spiritual success? One of the questions people ask often is, how do you know if your people are growing? How do you know if your groups are succeeding? Again, it depends on what your purpose is. Our purpose is to build significant Christian relationships. So that's the key measuring stick we use. That's why we have that mark of 80 percent in groups.

Again, we have this goal because we believe involvement in a group is one of the best spiritual growth environments we can put someone in. Now, that's a North Coast marker, not necessarily yours or the goal you need to or should be shooting for. Every church has its own context and history that plays into that. You as a church must decide the purpose of your small groups and set your own goals accordingly.

Spiritual Health vs. Spiritual Growth

I want to take a minute to talk about the discussion that so often comes up about evaluating spiritual growth. When someone asks me if someone is growing spiritually, I find it a bit difficult to answer. How do we define spiritual growth? Is it reading the Bible more? Spending more time at church? Being more articulate in our faith story? How often do you share your faith? All of those are good, but do they mean you're someone who is growing? They could be.

What about growing in Godly character? Now, that's a sign of growth, right? It's an example of the fruit of the Spirit working in them (Galatians 5:22, 23). I would agree; it's most likely a sign of growth. I've myself experienced and seen it. Yet, I repeatedly meet people who don't know Jesus but seem to have at least as much godly character or what we would call the "fruit of the Spirit," if not more than some long-time Christians I know.

It's confusing.

The answer became clearer as I watched the life and faith of a particular friend of mine unfold. We were in a group together for years. He knew the least amount of Scripture of anyone in the group, took the fewest notes during our weekend messages, and rarely did our group questions before the meeting. Yet what was interesting is that he was probably growing as much, if not more, spiritually than anyone in the group. He was owning his faith in new ways, engaging others to do the same. He was taking leadership and serving others. Some of those normal go-to markers of growing faith, like taking notes during sermons, studying his Bible on his own, and becoming articulate in deeper theology, were nonexistent in his life.

I also know that if I had told him to go to a Bible class on understanding his faith to help him grow, we may have lost him. Or at least I would have confirmed how painful some of those classes are for some. Classroom settings have never worked for him (even though he's a successful, longstanding tradesman and entrepreneur). Yet, his spiritual impact on others was significant. And here, years later, he does understand his faith more, continues to serve and impact, listens to our weekend messages, and still rarely takes notes or studies the Bible on his own. Yet, most weeks, he shows up to his life group.

Recently, I asked him if he likes to go to his life group. He said, "It's not always easy." And then he laughed.

Then I asked if he thought it was good for him to go. Without hesitation, he said, "Absolutely!"

At the life group, he dialogues with the rest of the group about life, and they talk about the sermon and some Bible verses that relate to it. He's motivated, encouraged, and challenged each week not to read his Bible more but to keep following Jesus and serving others as he has been. He also said that once he finishes this book, it will be the only one he's read in 25 years!

If someone grows spiritually, the typical evaluator asks, "Do they know the Bible better?" which is a great thing to have happen. But it does not mean they're growing spiritually, necessarily. It means they're growing in knowledge.

Most of us have encountered a person who knows the Bible well, but no one wants to be around them because of how they treat others. Or we've encountered people who know the Bible better than most but have vowed never to return to church.

Also, people don't typically grow on a linear track. Larry talks about it in his book *Sticky Church*, using the terms that people typically grow on a "need to know, need to grow" basis. He talks about how the lessons we learn are universal, but the order and how we learn them can differ greatly.

For example, one person who is interested in learning about the sovereignty of God may glean incredible insight into understanding it, while the next person may have no desire or need to dig into it. But if the next day, this disinterested person has someone close to them who is in a tragic accident, they are suddenly in a "need to know, need to grow" situation, trying to figure out how the sovereignty of God allowed this to happen.

This is also where the power of living in a community kicks in because the answer to them getting help is not typically to go study God's sovereignty. It's, "Do you have people around to help you with this, care for you, your friend, or their family, and process any questions you have about this?" If they then have questions about the sovereignty of God as it relates to their situation, in their connection with others, they can access those who can offer helpful knowledge about the topic in order to work through their spiritual questions. It was the *situation* that threw them into a "need to grow, need to know" stage of growth.

Without community, we're in trouble. That's why as a church, we are slow to put a measuring stick out there for people to evaluate their growth. We'd rather move the question from "Are you growing?" to "Are you spiritually healthy?"

But the question remains: how do you know if your groups and their people are spiritually healthy? Here are five vital signs that help us measure the health of our groups in providing an environment for growth for the people in them.

Vital Signs

Vital Signs of a Healthy Groups Ministry:

1. **% of adult weekend attendance in groups**: Our goal is to be 80% yearly. For the past 12 years, we've been at 90%+.

2. **Group attendance and retention:** Are people showing up to the group regularly and staying in the group long term? These are both important indicators of whether people are building significant relationships.

3. **Recruitment and retention of leadership**: Are we keeping or losing our leaders? We believe everything rises and falls on leadership. The question isn't whether we are losing any leaders, but rather, what's the percentage and why? (More on this in chapters 3 and 4)

4. **Group Signups**: Are we offering plenty of groups at multiple local locations in our community around the church on multiple days? People need options. Groups meeting on only one night of the week isn't offering groups to your entire church—it's only reaching the people who have that day and time open.

5. **Involved in Community Service**: We want to see at least 70 % of our groups involved in community service around the year. We work with partnership organizations throughout our community. You can learn more about how we do community service in Chapter 7.

These are vital statistics, and every year, we look at how we are doing. The purpose of these numbers is that they represent actual people. We want to be careful not to reduce people to just numbers but instead, to focus on the fact that the numbers represent our people. The remaining chapters will offer you strategies to see success in these areas. Once again, the primary question for you as a church is, what is the purpose of your groups? And how will you measure your results to know if your strategy is working?

NEXT STEPS STRATEGY: What do we need to need to start, stop, tweak, or keep?

Jot down what you need to remember as you look ahead, thinking through whom you need to bring to the table to talk about the purpose of your groups and possibly your entire church. This conversation will most likely help your church as a whole, and the various ministries sharpen their focus on what's important and maximize their effectiveness.

Now, take some time to work through the three variables to consider.

#1 How can you embrace your lead team or lead pastor's uniqueness, the vision for your church, and what the purpose of small groups at your church is?

#2 How does your church believe that spiritual growth happens? How will that help shape what your groups look like?

#3 Are you currently able to measure your group's success?

CHAPTER 3

Ask Someone

"We make a living by what we get, but we make a life by what we give."- Winston Churchill

"For we are God's handiwork created in Christ Jesus to do good works, which God prepared in advance for us to do." - Ephesians 2.10.

If you ask five people at your church who are followers of Jesus if they want to make a difference in the world, what do you think their answer will be? I'm leaning toward them saying yes, or at least they want to. Here's why: as followers of Jesus, we are naturally compelled to make a difference, thanks to the power of the Holy Spirit in us. As Ephesians 2:10 puts it, we are "created to do good works in Christ, which God prepared in advance for us to do." We are not saved by it, but we are created to do it (Ephesians 2:8, 9). And when we're not, we're not at our best or operating how we're designed.

Every follower of Jesus is set up to do things that impact the kingdom! If they say no to our question above, it's probably because they don't quite understand the question, it seems too big, or they have a distorted view of what it takes to make a difference (it's usually much simpler than they think). Jesus followers want to do ministry. And we, as leaders and pastors, have the opportunity and privilege to help them catch the vision of what the Holy Spirit is prompting them to do. But if this is the case, why is it challenging to find people to volunteer to lead our groups, or any other volunteer position for that matter?

Recruiting leaders is one of the most challenging things for a church leader to do (I know I'm preaching to the choir here). You were probably tempted to bypass all the other chapters and go directly to this one. I know I would be! You also know it's one of the most influential things you can do—multiplying impact. And without them, you know you're going nowhere.

Here at North Coast, we have a successful track record for recruiting leaders, but I'll be the first, and certainly not the last, to say it's not easy. You may have a vision that recruiting leaders for us is like picking apples off an apple tree—most of them are relatively easy to get, some are challenging because they're high and hard to see, but nothing a good ladder can't solve. But in the end, they are all right there for the pickin' (how I wish that were true, but nothing could be further from the truth!). Recruiting is the most challenging thing we do! In fact, some may say it's the biggest downside of our group's model because of the amount of work it takes based on our vetting process. That may be true. But I would say it's also our strength! I believe it's the most expansive, beneficial multiplier of our ministry abilities. It's helping people find their motivational sweet spot of God's spirit working through their own specially designed mix of gifts, skills, and experiences!

One of the greatest opportunities we have as Christian leaders is to help people see how they can use their gifts and abilities to further the Kingdom, reach and help people follow Jesus, and gain the support they need to continue.

So, why is it so challenging? Because as we've heard it said, "Anything worth much, costs much!" As your leadership goes, so goes your organization, and so goes your church. And if every organization rises and falls on leadership and is a direct reflection of it, the value is high along with the challenge.

Recruiting tends to be a strength of mine, but each year, I'm reminded that it's never easy. Though cultivating prospects for quality hosts and leaders is a year-round endeavor, August is our most crucial time to recruit leaders since our fall launch for groups is always the largest. I mention to my team every August, "Remind your family this is going to be a crazy time." This was one of the most significant changes I experienced moving into this role twenty years ago. Recruiting the right people costs time, and there are no 40-hour work weeks in August.

Potential leaders are typically available in the evenings and on the weekends, so that's when you will find most of our team making calls, following up on leads, and setting up meetings. I grew up on a farm in the Central Valley of California. When our peach orchards were ripe, it was picking season. All hands on deck, come rain or shine, before the sun was up and after it had gone down, the fruit needed to be picked. When it comes to recruiting leaders, August is our "Picking Season."

> **STAFF SKILL SIDEBAR**: Some of us are more comfortable with recruiting than others. From the start, when we look at who to bring onto your life group team, finding someone who is able to recruit and build teams is a high priority. It has to be; it's an essential part of the role. Just because someone knows the Bible, can speak up front, and administrate an event doesn't mean they can recruit. They need to have a track record of it. Even when recruiting young, less experienced staff, this is usually reflected in their relationships and hobbies at some level. And it isn't necessarily the typical extroverted "pied piper" leader, but also can be the more subtle networker and question-asker behind the scenes who quietly knows how to connect and then set a vision to help others jump in.

Here are **five principles** we live by to recruit and find the leaders and hosts we need.

#1 The Recruiting Pipeline

Learn to recruit by referral and not just by relationships. There are three typical ways to get volunteers to step up in leadership: ask your friends, ask for volunteers, or get referrals. Friends are great, but you'll never have enough. Plus, they'll start to avoid you if you ask too much. If you ask for volunteers, you will have conversations with individuals excited about this opportunity, but they may not actually be a good fit, and you may be left having a hard conversation. That doesn't feel good to anyone.

Conversely, if vetting your leadership isn't important, you end up dealing with the carnage of groups failing due to poor leadership. The third way is what we call referral-based recruiting. This is the method we use to go about finding our leaders. It allows you the opportunity to vet people right from the start based on the person giving the referral. It also enables you to create a much greater network of people looking for potential leaders.

Why the Mentor Multiplication Model Doesn't Work

One idea that seems to often be considered is that every group leader should find someone in their group to mentor as a future leader to then leave and launch another group later. It makes sense. We've tried it. It didn't work. Here's why:

First, we don't start groups just to split them or to get people to leave. We want people to build lifelong relationships that give them the support and encouragement they need over the long haul. We have plenty of groups that have been meeting for well over ten, even twenty years!

Second, the moment you ask a leader to mentor and "raise someone up," they suddenly have an additional task that makes their job more complicated. Whether they recognize it or not, every one of our leaders is mentoring and discipling their group simply by how they lead and engage their groups. Yet if you start with it on the front end as a given responsibility, your chances of getting them to lead decrease because you've grown the task. Most would anticipate this to entail extra meetings, conversations, and stress if they can't find someone or even overtly try. Leading a group every week is challenging enough.

For years, we worked hard on trying to get this model to work. It sounded good in theory. Yet, no matter how much we tried to simplify their view of mentoring, it still came across as a subtle fail if they weren't overtly engaging and developing someone to lead. The reality was they weren't failing. The failure was our strategy, not theirs.

And then it occurred to us that our leaders are no different than our staff. They all have great abilities, but they're not all recruiters. What if we change the paradigm from mentoring to simply asking for a referral? Instead of giving them the task of raising up or recruiting a leader, let's simply ask if they see anyone in their group with a possible leadership or hosting gene. It took the pressure off trying to get them to create vision and train up others to lead, and rather just look for potential leaders. Again, most were mentoring just by how they led and cared for their group. This was a game-changer for us in getting referrals and put less pressure on our leaders.

Five Pools for Referral-Based Recruiting

Pool #1 - Your Friends. We all have a group of friends. Never miss out on engaging those closest to you. You are the referral that allows you to ask them. And you never know when they may be thinking about new leadership opportunities you didn't know about. But also, don't miss out on asking them for referrals and to pray for you as you seek to find people to help launch groups. Though a valuable pool, it's probably also your smallest one, and chances are you won't have enough friends to find the number of leaders you need.

Pool #2 - Current Group Leaders & Hosts. Most of our referrals for leaders and hosts are from this pool, whether it's someone in their group or someone they know. Every meeting we have with our leaders, they hear us bring it up. "Are there any potential leaders or hosts you recommend from your group?" If they tell us they don't have any, we quickly ask the next question. "When you're not there, who leads your group?" Whoever they name is quickly placed on our referral list. Yet, it doesn't take long for our leaders and hosts to figure out that strategy and become slow to make recommendations because they don't want them to leave their group. They're an essential contributor to who their group is and what's happening within the group, which we understand. But we do need to keep the vision out there.

How Not to Split Groups, but Still Launch Leaders Out

Our leaders must know that we will never split or pull someone out of the group who doesn't want to or isn't ready to make a change to leading or hosting. We're trying to build lifelong friendships in the groups, not break up existing communities. We won't ever push anyone through a door to lead, leave a group, or start a new group if they shouldn't. But we also need to make sure they know that door is wide open for them to walk through if they want.

This means we need to make sure they know the opportunity is open. We don't want to be shy about inviting them to consider the opportunity if they'd like. If we don't, we could be blocking their view or even closing a door that they or the Holy Spirit may be prompting them to go through. Mentioning the opportunity to them, whether it's our staff or their own group leader, could be what allows them to start considering it. It's the Great

Commission (Matthew 28:19, 20): "Go into all the world and make disciples." We never want to hinder someone from fulfilling that calling and moving into a new role.

We remind our leaders how they were approached by someone (and the Holy Spirit) at some point who thought they would be good at leading or hosting a group. Some of them were ready to jump, and others were unsure. But because someone mentioned it to them, they began to consider a move into a new role.

There are reasons why a potential new leader shouldn't leave a group. When a leader says, "I have some people who could lead, but they can't leave our group," we ask what's going on; why not? At times, they may have a sensitive issue the group is dealing with, and the potential leader is essential in helping offer the needed support with what's happening. Or a current leader might miss regularly due to work obligations, and they need this other person to lead when they aren't there.

Our affirmation and understanding in these cases are important. We need to trust our leaders and their judgment. Our respect and trust in them will help them continue to lead over the long haul and give us referrals as we move forward.

Launching leaders or hosts from an existing group

There are three way we suggest doing this:

- New leader or host leave the group to launch new group
- New leader or host take over existing group and existing leader leaves to start new group
- Group divides and creates two new groups

Pool #3 – Former leaders. These are the leaders who took a step back from leading. When someone steps down, although we understand, it can be disappointing. But what we've learned is that if we respect their decision to step down and take a break graciously, there's a good chance they may come back. I remember a leader apologizing for wanting to take a break. This person had been leading for eleven straight years! My response at that moment was far from disappointment (I've grown over the years); but rather, we need to give them an award for staying with it that long! And not surprisingly, it was just a couple of years later that they were back. They just needed some time off. They should never feel pushback from us in these cases, but rather a thank you! And yes, we often find leaders ready to jump back in because they're natural leaders. The Holy Spirit is at work, and they are compelled to lead.

Pool #4 – Staff and volunteer rosters. So, you've asked your friends, you've asked your current leaders, you've asked your former leaders, and you still need some more names. Another option is to check with your staff. I don't mean just walking by and asking them or sending an email to see if they have any suggestions. That's putting the work on them to make referrals, and no one has time for that. We must do the work to make it doable for others to work. Here's the process we go through when asking staff for referrals. We ask if we can meet for about 5-10 minutes to review their volunteer roster to see if they have any referrals for potential leaders and hosts. Next, if you can, get the roster yourself or have them do it, and just sit down and read through the names to see if there is anyone they would recommend as a potential leader or host. I've sat with each of our executive and children's ministry teams repeatedly over the years, and as we read through it, they would point out a name, I would put a checkmark on it, and ask a few questions about who they are and why they are recommending them. In that short time span, we almost always came up with more names than I could have imagined. And it usually took considerably less effort than the staff member thought.

> **Why Stealing Volunteers from Other Ministries is OK**
>
> Some of you may be wondering, "Wait a minute. How is your staff willing to give you referrals from their volunteers? Aren't you stealing them from their ministries?" Fortunately in our case at North Coast, we're not actually stealing them and here's why. We intentionally refrain from scheduling any other ministry activities (aside from junior high, high school, and young adult youth groups) during the week in order to keep people's schedule available to attend, lead, or host a life group. I discuss the philosophy behind this more in Chapter 5 in the section titled "Understand the Competition."

Pool #5 - Previous No's. What do we do when they tell us no? Another pool of people to recruit from are those who previously told you no. Once we get a referral from someone, whether they tell me yes or no, they will continue to be a ministry partner with me.

Let me explain. A typical response when someone tells us no is that we're disappointed and move on. Totally normal. But don't do it! Let me play this out some more. Once they tell me no, my next questions are important. Their response may have been, "I'm coaching a Little League team this year." At this point, if you're like me, I have to fight off the idea in my mind that leading one of our groups is more important than them coaching Little League. But is it? We need Christians involved in Little League out in the community, don't we? Of course, we do. Our goal can't be to just fill a slot for OUR ministry; it's to help find a ministry God has called them to. And for someone, at least for that point in time, that might be a little league coach. If they hear us giving up on them just because they told us no, that's not a good sign. That's not authenticity. We want to stay engaged in who they are and affirm what God has for them. If they've been referred to you by someone else, that person believes that this referral has some leadership game!

When they tell you what's going on for them, little league coach, caring for an aging parent, or whatever it might be, jot it down. I need to track these details if I really want to build and maintain a relationship with them. And then I would say, "You know how important our groups are at North Coast to help people stay connected. Could you take the next few days and pray for us to be able to find some new leaders and also talk to your spouse or friends about anyone they might recommend leading or hosting a group? I could give you a call in a few days to see if you came up with any ideas. And no problem if you can't think of any." Most people are willing to do that. They've just become your ministry partner!

The final thing I mention is that, if it's okay with them, I'll call them back in six months to a year and see where they're at. I called Tom four years in a row. "This is your annual call!" I'd say, and we'd laugh together. We'd talk and catch up. I couldn't help but be a bit surprised in that fourth year when he said "yes" to him and his wife leading a group. They ended up leading a group for the next five years and saw lives changed. It was clearly the ministry God had for them at that season of their life.

We Can't Microwave Leadership

It can't be about getting people to just say yes right now! It has to be about building trust and understanding how life works and who people are. I hope that when you're told no, you continue to look at the bigger picture and how God may want to still use them in some capacity in your ministry, and if not, this is your opportunity to encourage them in a ministry that God may have for them.

Special Note About Contacting Referral Leads: Encourage them!

When we share that we got a recommendation for them to lead, it needs to be an encouragement to them. It's saying someone believes in them, so it's important you're communicating that. Also, we never cold call. The potential future leader always gets an email, note, or text from me first sharing that they've been recommended as a leader, and I'd love to talk to you. I'll give you a call in a few days to talk over some options that could work for you. Feel free to reach out sooner if you'd like. Notice that we're not asking them if we can call. We don't want them to be making a decision about leading before we can talk first.

#2 Shared Leadership Makes Everyone Better (Leaders and Hosts)

There are several biblical examples that display this principle. Jesus sent the disciples and the seventy-two "out two by two" (Mark 6:7; Luke 10:1). Ecclesiastes 4:9-10 speaks of "two are better than one because they have a good reward for their toil." None of these are biblical imperatives for small-group leadership, but the principle is clear—there is power in two. We found the same to be true – our groups are stronger, and our leaders last longer when they are partnered in leadership. Here's how teaming together makes them better.

- *Encouragement.* It's no easy task to lead a group week in and week out. Encouraging words and feedback are valuable along the way for all of us.

- *Share the load.* There are many tasks beyond just leading the group discussion. Following up and caring for specific needs of individuals, having a place to meet and getting it ready, planning the social and community service project, weekly desserts, etc. We consider the hosts as leaders also, but use a different name to help establish their differing roles.

- *Perspective and accountability.* This is similar to the reality that we're all typically better humans when mom is in the room. Other leaders in the room help us stay on task, consider more closely how we lead, confirm our perspective, or give us another one.

What we have also found is that the most effective leader-host team is when they are from two different families. This means not just a husband and wife with one taking on the leader role and the other the host role.

Some married friends of mine who are long-time experienced leaders began to think our value of shared leadership from different families was limiting us from finding new leaders to launch more groups. So, they decided to encourage their host to venture out and launch a new group. They solved their missing host issue by simply having one of them remain in the lead role and the other take on the normal responsibilities of the host. Fully satisfied in helping us "launch more groups" and maintaining our shared leadership value, off they went to start a new quarter with their group.

It took them just a few weeks to realize it was a mistake. They had to do everything it took to get their group going at the level they used to. The value of shared leadership from different families suddenly became incredibly apparent—they had no idea how good they had it and were now missing the encouragement, partnership, and the importance of another set of humans to keep perspective as the group met from week to week. They wasted no time making sure they had another host as soon as they could because they knew it would keep them fresher to lead and receive the encouragement they needed.

Do we ever launch groups without hosts or without someone from another family? At times we do make exceptions, but we always want a host to be raised up within their group by the end of the quarter. Also, the role of the host doesn't mean it has to be in the host's home. Though it typically is, it can be in the leader's home or even someone else who is in the group. See the Additional Resource Section (at the end of the book) for job descriptions of Leaders and Hosts.

#3 Clarity and Personal Contact

Clearly communicate your vision and expectations. We meet with every leader before we ask them to lead. It's here where we hear their story, get a sense of who they are, and share the purpose of our groups. It's invaluable time spent. The memory of those meetings is lasting because of the personal connection that occurs when hearing their story of life change, and for some, taking their first step in leading adults spiritually. This meeting also tells the leaders from the beginning that we're available. It's here we clearly share that they can contact us anytime they need help and begin explaining what it means to lead a group and how we define success. The intent of our group meetings is to build friendships that offer the support of a life centered on Jesus, not just a Bible study.

I should add that we typically don't meet one-on-one to interview our hosts. We do vet them the same as leaders regarding needing a referral and sending out an "all staff leader flag check" to see if there are any extra affirmations or concerns (explained in the "Six Questions We Ask" section later in this chapter). To match leaders with hosts, we usually ask both if there is anyone they'd like to team up with to launch the group that isn't already hosting or leading. Sometimes, they say they do but are concerned about asking them because they are in another group.

We are quick to respond with that's not an issue. Someone leaving a group that isn't already leading or hosting to step up into a new leadership role could be a great next step for them. If they can't find someone, we get busy finding a pairing that will work. Ensuring a good fit is an important next step. Once we find someone, we suggest a short get-together for coffee or dessert to see if the needed chemistry between them is there, and then ask each to individually get back to us as staff and let us know if it's a go. Hearing back from each one is important. It almost always is a go.

When it comes to time commitment, we try to keep it as simple as possible. There's a one-time new leader training we ask our leaders and hosts to attend (in-person or online). And then, only once a year, we'll ask you to meet at a time they're not already at church. It's our annual kickoff for our leaders and hosts. There are only two others, but we make them very doable. We offer those at our weekend services when you're already there. And here's what else we'll have at every meeting: a meal and free childcare (more on this in Chapter 4).

We know that many of our new leaders will have some fear around dealing with tough issues and questioning how well they know the Bible. We've created easy-to-access "real-time" resources. The first one is our personal phone number to call or text anytime they need help or have a question. The other is our weekly guide, which they can access online as a podcast or written doc to help them lead their group that week (more on that in chapters 4 and 6).

#4 No One Is Better Than the Wrong One

There are different views on who should be in leadership and who shouldn't. We obviously vet our leaders. They don't have to be at the church planter level or have high Bible knowledge, but they do need to have a good reputation, character, and some ability to either lead, facilitate, or shepherd. Without the vetting process, the fallout from a group led poorly can come at a high cost.

Every year, I hear people (usually guys) share their fear of joining a group. They're afraid they will be asked questions they don't know how to answer and are a bit concerned about what kinds of emotions will be shared. We get it. Poorly and non-prepared leadership in a group can confirm all these fears, ensuring they most likely won't return or be willing to give another group a try in the future.

#5 Be Willing to Pay the Price

A principle we live by is that we want to do the hard work so our leaders can do effective work. I don't want you to miss this. Hard work in the garden before the fall was a joy. Taking the time to come alongside and recruit, to help people find how they can use their gifts and abilities to build relationships to make a difference, is no doubt hard work. But the reward is significant, not just for them as individuals but also as a role model for their family and friends. Working hard on these principles on the front end has also proven to keep our leaders longer. Also, doing what it takes to recruit leaders for the long haul is much less work than having to do it again to replace them the next year.

Six Questions We Ask to See if Someone Is Ready to Lead or Host:

1) *Have they been a follower of Jesus for at least a year?*

A year may seem long to some and short to others. Again, the leader who made the referral is helping you understand the maturity of this referral. There is no date set in Scripture for how long someone needs to be waiting, but it does say it needs to not be a new believer (1 Timothy 3:6). There does need to be visible fruit and consistency to their spiritual walk regardless of how long they have been a believer.

2) *Are there any issues that our staff or lead team are aware of?*

The more we can figure out if someone is the right fit before we talk to them, the better the interview is going to go. When we get a referral, the first thing we do is look at their involvement in the church and send out to our entire staff what we call a Leadership Flag Check. Here's how it reads:

Subject line: Life Group leader flag check.

Text: Thank you for any thoughts or feedback on these people. Please keep this inquiry confidential as we're waiting for feedback before we contact them.

Name listed

Thanks,
Dave Enns

Our entire team knows that when they see an email with that subject, they need to take a look at it right away. If they have any concerns (or extra affirmations), they give us a call or send an email back and ask us to check with them. We do that for every individual. We wait 24 hours to give the team time to respond before we reach out to the potential leader or host. We have found this vital for our vetting process. Knowing our entire staff has been asked about this builds our confidence in recruiting them to a leadership position. Most responses are affirmations. But when they're not, it is incredibly helpful for the next steps. And if you're the only staff person, include your lead volunteers. All our ministries now use the same process in recruiting volunteers due to its effectiveness.

3) *Do they have a track record and a commitment to integrity, Godly character, and spiritual growth?*

This is a crucial part of the initial referral process and the "flag check email" I spoke of above. When getting a referral, this question is part of the discussion about this person. Since we meet with all of our potential new leaders one-on-one for an interview, we also get their faith story and talk through these expectations. This also allows us to get a better feel for their ability to be warm and friendly. This intangible is an important part of creating an inviting, friendly environment.

4) *Have they been in a group for at least a quarter?*

This is helpful in two ways. First, in the vetting process, getting referrals from people who have seen them in the group, how consistent they are, how they listen, how they deal with conflict, and how they interact is gold. Second, it's key in helping people understand how we do groups. The assumptions, expectations, and experiences of what groups should look like are diverse. That's why even if someone comes with experience in leading a small group in another setting, they may not understand how we do groups.

We tell them we'd love to see that become an option. What we'd like you to do is join a group, and then we'll talk after the quarter. Now, let's be real. That's not easy to say for any of us. We always want and need more leaders. Yet, it's surprising to me that it's not odd that we find out that if they are extra pushy on this, they would not have been a good fit to lead after all. When high impatience occurs at this initial stage, be careful. What we have found is the ones who communicate impatience usually lack a leadership quality that's important to a group's success.

We also do this when we bring on new Life Group staff, even if they have group leadership experience or expertise. We typically team them up with a veteran staff member who's leading a group. For that first quarter, they oftentimes are in two groups - one they are in and one they lead. Everyone that has done it was thankful we did, even though they were surprised it's what we wanted them to do. And for those moving in from out of the area, it gives them an extra quick dose of connection.

Do we ever make an exception? Yes, on occasion. There are three situations when we do. One is when we're launching a new campus, the second is when we're launching groups online outside of our area, and the third is when a campus is experiencing exponential growth. The first two are straightforward because there's no prior campus in each of those settings; no one could have been in a group prior. Yet in each case, we keep the same vetting process minus the requirement to have been in a group for a quarter.

5) *Do they have one of the three following skills—leading, shepherding, or facilitating?*

I'm sure you've come across people who have leadership qualities, but they themselves just don't see it. Perhaps they have a limited view of what qualifies someone as a leader.

When recruiting, we say we're looking for one of three skills to lead a group—typical leading abilities, shepherding, or facilitating. It's also why when you visit groups, they often run differently—in one group, the strength of the leader is obvious. They are the ones taking charge and making things happen.

In the next group, the leader may be less overt but clearly the one helping everyone engage at a high level. This leader's outstanding strength is facilitating.

The next group may not seem as focused, but there's no doubt how much they are being cared for. The strength of this leader is a shepherd. Typically, most leaders have at least some of all three but may need help balancing what they lack. We work on developing all three of these skills as we train. It's also why teaming them up as a host leadership team, as we talked about earlier, is so important because you're meshing those gifts together. It's the beauty of shared leadership.

6) *Do they have friends?*

The question we're asking here is, do they have the social skills or relational warmth to lead and/or host a group? Do people like being around them? They don't have to be like the Pied Piper and have people follow them wherever they go, but do they have a friend group?

Let me say a little more about this because we need to be careful not to confuse someone we don't connect with with someone who does not have the social skills to lead or host. I remember when I came into this role years ago, a person leading a group that I was surprised was leading. He had strong character, cared for people, loved Jesus, and was a little odd at times. I didn't know how his leadership piece worked. I loved him but just didn't click with who he was.

To my surprise, his groups thrived! Part of his success was due to his spouse and the hosts in the group. But as I watched and heard from people in the group, he was the key reason they were in their group and staying. It was a great reminder to me that I'm not looking for people like me but people that others like!

You've heard how we go about training our leaders and the reasons why. Below are the four questions we considered as we created our model:

---

4 Areas to consider when setting your leadership bar:

- Bible Knowledge - How much scripture do they need to know?
- Spiritual Maturity - How mature do they need to be?
- Ministry Experience - What skills do they need to have & at what level?
- Training - Are there trainings they need to attend?

Recruiting Process

NEXT STEPS STRATEGY: What do we need to need to start, stop, tweak, or keep?

Based on what you read above, are there any adjustments you want to make on how you recruit and vet new leaders and hosts?

What does your job description look like for your leaders and hosts? Do you need to create one? Any changes you need to make to the ones you have?

What questions are important for you of those that you are considering for a leadership position?

What is the minimum bar for leadership within your church? Do different positions have different bars to meet?

CHAPTER 4

Equip Someone

"Men and women want to do a good job, a creative job, and if they are provided the proper environment, they will do so." - Bill Hewlett

"Christ himself gave the Apostles, the Prophets, the evangelists, the pastors, and teachers to equip his people for works of service so that the body of Christ may be built up until we all reach unity and faith in the knowledge of the Son of God and become mature, attaining to the whole measure of the fullness of Christ." - Ephesians 4:11-13.

In this chapter, you and your leaders will be empowered to work smarter, not harder or longer, while sleeping better and accomplishing more! Do I have your attention? It's a bold claim, but I think I can get you there.

It was my third year in college, sitting in one of my Christian education classes. As my professor was talking about churches, church growth, and making a difference, he said something I'll never forget. "Pastors often think their church isn't growing because of the people. But it's often the leader's inability to adapt as the ministry is growing or the culture around them is changing that is hindering them." Though there was plenty I don't remember from that class, this I did! It caught my attention because I had already seen it happen repeatedly. And I did not want to be that guy.

Fast forward to my fifth year leading our college ministry here at North Coast. The ministry started with five guys in my apartment. There were now 100 showing up weekly, and more joining regularly. It was thriving. And my professor's words were still ringing in my ears. What do I need to do to ensure I don't get in the way of this? I don't want to be that guy!

I was a relational leader with an organizational ability. But our growth meant I could no longer depend on my relational strength to lead the charge in growing our ministry. The question that loomed over me was, am I adapting and changing to meet the demands of a growing ministry? I wasn't sure that I was or that I even knew how to. I felt paralyzed. It wasn't for a lack of information available to me; it was that I had too much information. My degree was in Christian education. At that stage in my ministry career, I was well-read in the latest ministry leadership books and had been to plenty of conferences, all adding to my list of what "I needed to do" to NOT be "that guy"! But everyone had a different opinion, a different strategy, a different does and don'ts list. It was overwhelming.

The enemy was doing all he could to say, "There's too much; you don't have what it takes; you ARE that guy!" I was beyond myself, and this is often when God does His best work in us. Through prayer and wise counsel, I began to let others in on my struggle. I brainstormed with my friends and leaders around me on how to simplify this list. I wanted to ensure I was adapting my leadership style and equipping our leaders and team with all they needed to be effective, not holding back what God seemed to be moving forward.

Through that process, I came up with what I believe was transformational in focusing my time, energy, and confidence on the things that we needed to build and empower a team of volunteers and leaders without burning out. I refer to it as the "Four Es of Influence" (*Empower, Equip, Evaluate, and Encourage*).

Over the next five years, we saw our college ministry triple in size in attendees and volunteers. Since moving into our lead position of groups here at North Coast, now 20 years ago, we have grown from 2,000 people in groups to now over 8,000 while seeing our volunteer leadership base mirror the same growth. We now have over 1,500 leaders and hosts. I am a bit cautious about sharing these numbers with you because we so quickly move to the comparison or competition game as to who's the best and who isn't.

The reason I share this with you is I want you to know what worked for us and that it's scalable to any size ministry. Your time is your most valuable commodity, and I hope it helps you focus on where to put your energy and expand your outcomes. As I said earlier, raising up leaders is our biggest multiplier of impact. It not only applies to training small group leaders but any leadership setting you're in. Even parenting! I often see training that is well-intentioned but wastes time, energy, and focus because we treat leaders like followers, unaware of what they really need and want.

My hope is it helps you be more effective and efficient. Ironically, what you'll see is many of the terms and practices I refer to won't be new to you but rather offer a focused strategy and process to empower and equip your team, ministry, or business to effectively thrive and grow over the long haul without burning you or them out.

The Four E's of Influence

It's four principles that, if practiced over and over again with the people we lead, direct, and care for, will offer them all they need to stay motivated and effective!

1) Empower through Vision.

Casting vision is vital. It unleashes the individual with a bigger purpose and passion for the task and keeps them going when they hit the wall. And everyone hits the wall! In everything we do, at some point, we hit a roadblock, lose desire, energy, and no longer want to push through.

As kids, we don't want to continue to go to school, but we push through because our parents are setting the vision (and discipline) that we need to get an education. There are plenty of days for all of us when we don't want to go to work, yet we push through because we have the vision that it's good to get paid. As followers of Jesus, we are offered the grandest vision, purpose, and motivation by how we live, as we have the opportunity to represent Jesus to others, no matter what our situation is, and even get an eternal reward for it (Colossians 3:23, 24)! We are, in a sense, walking Bibles of God's love, grace, and forgiveness based on how we interact with those around us. Now, that gives us vision and purpose as followers of Jesus, no matter where we live or what we have. Vision is what gets us going, keeps us going, and gives us purpose in what's before us!

When I'm training our new leaders and hosts, I confess to them that there are plenty of times I don't want to go to my life group. They're surprised because it's what I'm supposed to be all about! That's true, but it is reality. Of course, they get it because they all deal with the same thing. And then I share with them why I still go (besides the fact it's part of my job). This goes back to Hebrews 10:24, 25, and the vision it creates to motivate me to show up when I don't want to.

When you gather, you're encouraging each other to love and do good deeds, to keep the faith, and keep loving others when it just ain't easy—It's a holy moment! Every time we meet and circle up, we build relationships, trust, and the ability to hear the Holy Spirit speak, not just to me, but through other people to me and from me to them and God's Word to us. It's an incredible trifecta experience resulting from the "circle effect" creating a circular or self-perpetuating impact. It's why I go, even when I don't feel like it.

As leaders, we have to cast vision all the time, over and over again, wherever we are. That's an important part of our job. Wouldn't it be great if we only had to say it one time? That's not how it works. Not for our leaders, not for any of us. That's why Jesus said, "Do this in remembrance of me." He knows we all need to hear it over and over again because we all forget! We all lose sight of it. The message in Proverbs 29:18 states it this way, "If people can't see what God is doing, they stumble all over themselves." Vision keeps us motivated and on track!

I remember recruiting a new leader, and after his group's second meeting, he gave me a call. The previous leader of the group had left, and he had taken on the leadership role. He was a bit reluctant but believed in the vision of what we were trying to accomplish.

When I answered the phone, I could tell right away something was wrong. His frustration was palpable as he explained that a couple joined their group, and they were talking about getting a divorce. His frustration was actually fear. He had no idea how to handle this but felt responsible for solving it. He felt that he was way over his head.

I quickly responded, "I want you to know that I'm here to help you with this, but I also want to let you know I'm so glad they're in your group."

His response was quick and full of disbelief. "What do you mean you're so glad they're in our group (now sounding more annoyed with me than when he did earlier)? I can't deal with this."

I said, "I understand; that is challenging. I want you to know I'm here to help. You don't have to deal with this on your own. Here's why I said I'm glad they're in your group. Imagine with me for a second if this couple didn't join a group and they didn't have someone like you calling someone like me that can help bring some resources to help give them the best shot at working this out and maybe keeping them together."

He responded, "I didn't even think about that. I so needed to hear that."

He was hitting the wall (understandably), and the vision of what being in a group means was now helping him break through the wall. He was now back on track, seeing the value of his role and seeing how he could make a difference in what looked to be an impossible situation.

That's what vision casting does. Everybody hits the wall at some point, so we've got to cast vision everywhere all the time. Every time we lead a meeting, we need to be casting a vision that ties in with the bigger purpose. Vision is what motivates us when times get hard and can keep us moving forward.

You'll hear at North Coast these words or concepts over and over again—connection, connection, connection—we're consistently and repeatedly casting vision for the power and importance of connection. In fact, if we haven't heard something about our life groups and connection in our weekend message three weeks in a row, I have the green light to bring it up to our teaching Pastors! This is because we see relationships and connection as essential to spiritual health and growth and can't be unattached to what it means to be following Jesus! Larry calls it the drip method. (More on that in Chapter 5). Our kickoff event for all leaders and hosts is fully focused on setting vision and commissioning our leaders as we launch into a new life group year.

2) Equip for the Ministry.

Here, we focus on making sure our leaders have the tools, training, and expectations they need to be successful. Vision alone won't do it. And here's why it's important. They give your leaders a track to run on to be successful.

I love this quote from Bill Hewlett, "Men and women want to do a good job, a creative job, and if they are provided the proper environment, they will do so." It is for this reason that if we bring someone into leadership and they fail, we consider it our fault, not theirs. We don't have to tell them to be successful or even encourage them in that way—being successful is already part of their plan. But that doesn't mean they know what success is or how to get there. So that is where we train and guide them.

One thing to keep in mind as you guide them is that they don't need to be the best leader ever. In fact, we have no need or goal for them to be the best; we just need our leaders to be "good enough" to get the job done. Of course, no one wants to be a failure either, but there is a chasm between failing, being good enough, and being the best. So that's our goal—we want to offer our leaders the tools, training, and expectations they need to be good enough—because it's all we need! Here's what we do to equip them.

Setting Expectations

There are essentially two expectations that we set for our leaders. The first is character. Character and integrity in leadership are nonnegotiable, which is why our vetting process is so critical. Having strong character and maintaining integrity doesn't mean leaders can't or don't have real struggles. They do. Sometimes, they may need help with their marriage, family, finances, work, etc. Character allows them to be willing to see their struggle and get the help they need. There are times a leader may need to step back from their role to be able to give the time and focus needed to work on a significant issue, but that's all part of us as staff coming alongside and helping them work it out.

The second expectation is the ability to lead their group by having a commitment to building Christian relationships within the group and keeping God's word at the center. This happens through the sharing of life, studying the Word, supporting each other through life's events, and serving others as Christ has served us. It is the expectation of the leader to create an environment through leading, shepherding, or facilitating for their group to grow.

Tools and Training—Reachable Resources and Real-Time Training Rhythm

One of the key questions asked when someone is joining a leadership team is how much extra time it is going to take to prepare to lead the group and how many meetings they will have to add to their schedule. We work hard at not making them extra busy. We offer three meetings a year, and only one is going to take time out of their normal schedule. It's our leader kickoff meeting for the year that typically happens on Friday night. Everyone loves it. The other two happen when they're already at church during the weekend services. There is also a new leader training they attend just once. At all our meetings, we offer free childcare and a meal.

Right now, you're saying, "Wait a minute. That's going to cost the church money." Last I checked, quality leadership always does. And we do get what we pay for! Food is a relational gatherer, and a thank you for showing up, and childcare enables your leadership to attend without having to pay up!

There are two other on-demand resources you can access anytime you want—a weekly leaders guide and access to their Pastor anytime extra help is needed. We sum all this up by calling it the "1-3-30-24/7" resource which translates to:

- 1 New Leader Training (one-time)
- 3 Leadership Community Gatherings (yearly)
- 30 Real-time leader Guides (available weekly)
- 24/7 – On-demand Coaching (whenever needed)

Here's what each of these resources specifically looks like:

1 New Leader Essentials Training

This is where we train our leaders how to lead their group and how to hear from everyone every time they meet. The goal is to ask questions and not be advice givers – they're not counselors. Not only are our leaders not expected to act as counselors, but they are also, in fact, discouraged from acting like one. We train our new leaders to deal with any problem that ever comes out just by asking four simple questions. (See Chapter 6 for more details on the Four Qs.) The leaders' goal is not to instruct but rather facilitate a conversation and ask questions, which also opens the door wider for them to lead well. We also train our leaders to have a great first meeting with their people because it's that first meeting that is going to set up how their group is going to operate for the next 10 weeks. (more on this in Chapter 6)

3 Leadership Community Gatherings

1) Life Group Leader / Host Kickoff:

This is a vision and commissioning event for all leaders and hosts. We host Kickoff the week before we launch our new year in groups during the fall. It's similar to a pep rally before the big game. It usually includes dinner, a mingler, worship, a brief vision casting, and a commissioning message. There is always an emphasis on how their time and effort is going to make a difference.

This event is as much of a thank you and encouragement as it is vision casting. Depending on the size of your organization, a Kickoff event can take on many variations. If you have a small group of leaders, it could be as simple as a barbecue in someone's backyard or, with a larger group, a full-blown worship and encouragement event on your church campus. You decide. We've added, at times, plenty of fun skits by our youth team, wild performances, and memorable photo booths that help our leaders laugh and enjoy their time together. This is a would-not-want-to-miss type of event focused on how God has brought everyone there with the opportunity to build transformational relationships. We communicate that this vision is not possible without our leaders.

2) Mid-Quarter Leadership Gatherings:

The other two gatherings are what we would call mid-quarter training leadership gatherings. They typically happen during our weekend services, so leaders can choose the one service time they typically go to without having to change their family schedule. And yes, because this training happens during a weekend service, childcare is already taken care of. Win, win! It works fantastically. And if you question, "Well, doesn't that mean your leaders are skipping out on a weekend sermon?!" Yes, and our weekend teaching team is in full support of this.

Remember, these people are your leaders. Sermons are readily available online or at another service time if they choose. They are capable. Years ago, we used to offer our mid-quarter training only during one service. When we ran out of room for one of our meetings, we realized we needed to expand the option to the second service. We were initially disappointed because we couldn't have all the leaders in the same room. But as soon as we added the second service option, we found out more leaders were showing up because they didn't have to change what service they were going to. Attending the training was more realistic because it wasn't an extra ask. And our training actually ended up being more personal and interactive because of the smaller size. Below is what those meetings typically contain.

How to Make a Mid-Quarter Training Great!

- *Inspire*: Cast vision and tell stories of changed lives—here's how what you're doing is making a difference

- *Inspect*: Feedback on what's going well and how they're being challenged.

- *Instruct*: Interactive and reality-based—adding to their leadership tool chest. Make sure you move from the principle to the real-life how-to, i.e., what this would really look like in action in their Life Group meeting. Have them leave with more than they came with. We not only want to train them to be better small group leaders, but better in life overall.

- *Inform:* Gathering and delivering insider info, important dates, potential leaders, attendance records, etc. The ultimate compliment we receive is, "Can you send me your notes so I can use them for my next business staff training meeting? I wish they would do training like this at my work!"

> **Two items you need to provide for all Leader Meetings:** Food and free childcare. (Food is one of the great connectors and relaxers of people. And because our leaders are frontline pastors, that's why we're always willing to do this. I remember years ago, when the dot com crash happened, our budgets got tight, just like everyone else's. Did we continue to feed our leaders at our meetings? You bet we did. Did they look a little different? They did during that time. But we were still committed to it. The next one is childcare. If you don't provide free childcare during your training meeting, chances are you're only going to get one parent, if any, and it places an extra high burden on the single parent. Not offering it makes that meeting cost a lot more than just time. I think I offer some quality training to our leaders. But it is probably not good enough to charge our volunteer leaders an entrance fee.

30-Real-Time Resource Options for Your Leaders

Every week, we provide our leaders with a valuable resource called the weekly leader guide for their group gathering. We follow a sermon-based model, but even if you're not in that setting, a simple, short-bulleted weekly update on the flow of meetings and rhythm of group tips and thoughts as they progress could be helpful. The guide provides additional questions, tips, and techniques to help them lead their group gathering that week.

We understand that some leaders naturally know how to add additional questions to encourage communication among their group members, while others may struggle. Our leader's guide offers them a few extra questions and scriptures they can reference if desired, along with addressing any specific concerns, offering guidance, and suggesting directions to take and avoid. I know that sounds complicated, but it really isn't. It's just putting on paper what you intuitively and naturally do when you lead a group.

By offering that to others, it could be a game-changer for your leaders. Let me explain why. When I first stepped into this role, 30% of our leaders were accessing what was then a 12 to 15-minute audio guide on a CD they picked up at our weekend services. I began to wonder if it was worth the effort to produce each week with that few paying attention to it.

During one of our leaders' meetings, I approached a highly capable leader and asked if he used it. To my surprise, he answered, "Yes, every week."

I couldn't understand why he needed it when he was already skilled and experienced in leading his group. So, I asked, "But you don't really need it, right?

He replied, "Well, not necessarily, but I still use it every week."

I was puzzled and asked him what he would do if we stopped offering it. He said, "I would quit."

I couldn't comprehend why he would quit if he didn't need it. He explained, "Dave, every person you recruit is busy. I think you know by now they are the only individuals who sign up to lead. You're right. I don't have to have it, but it serves as a 'tickler file' to get me thinking and helps me focus on the questions I should be asking."

In that moment, I realized we would never stop providing the leader's guide, even if only 30% of our leaders were accessing it.

Over the next year, I began to ask the question of what would happen if we offered it as a written guide also. Would more people access it? At that point, we weren't online. They were picking up CDs with audio at the weekend services. We decided to give it a try for a quarter, and if it didn't get much use, we could always stop. We also wanted to offer it with a quick reference feel with easy-to-see tips and extra questions and not offer it as verbatim of the audio. To our surprise, the users skyrocketed to 70% almost immediately.

Seventeen years later, it's still accessed by 70% of our leaders! It's now online and offered as a podcast, PDF, and a Word doc. It's an indispensable tool for our leaders. And here's something else that I didn't realize at first. It's another key element in recruiting and keeping our leaders over the long haul. It addresses their concerns about knowing how to lead a discussion, how well they know the Bible, and tips on how to get their group to engage and deal with potential issues. And because it's real-time every week, it communicates that we're available if you need us. We remind them of that almost every week in the introduction. See Life Group Leader Tools in the Additional Resource Section.

24/7 On-Demand Coaching

One of the significant roadblocks to recruiting leaders and hosts is the challenge of dealing with people and problems—small or large. And here's what we tell them. Never fear; we are here. Here's my cell phone—a direct line to me. Call me anytime if you have a question or find yourself in a situation where you're not sure what to do or how to engage it, small or large. I've had many people surprised we'd give our personal info out to that many people, especially in our church our size, assuming our cell phone and text would be non-stop. That has never been the case. There are a couple of reasons why.

First, remember what I said about leaders. The group of people leading your groups are leaders, not followers. Generally speaking, they have the ability to think on their feet and have good judgment—you and someone else have already confirmed that. They will not need to call for smaller issues because they are capable and they know.

Second, we have also trained them that their role is not to solve everyone's problems or have all the answers, but rather do what they can to bring the resources and support individuals need by asking questions. These questions are part of our training, so they are equipped to use them when the time arises.

3) Evaluate for success.

Every healthy relationship or organization creates an avenue for feedback, both positive and negative. Our intent has to be advocacy, not critique, as we know the leaders want to be successful. We let our leaders know we're here to help with whatever they need, especially if they find something challenging. At the end of each quarter, all members of our groups are sent feedback forms about their group experience. Here's how this kind of feedback is helpful and why it's important.

- *It keeps the individual focused on the right priorities.*

We offer a leader's guide every week for their group that reminds them of the priority of hearing from everyone every time they meet and keeping

God's word at the center. We also cover this extensively in our new leader training, coaching them on how to accomplish this. If their feedback forms come back with a concern regarding group discussion, then we have an open door to check in with the leader about how their discussions are going. The weekly attendance we receive from every group offers us indicators of what's happening in the group. It also allows us to check in with the leaders to see if they need any support, encouragement, or help with how the group is going and focusing on the right priorities.

- *It gives the individual the opportunity to give you feedback regarding their needs.*

If attendance is the problem, we can then check in to see what's happening, and the leader can communicate that they need help knowing how to respond. It could be as simple as learning to follow up with those who missed the meeting with a kind message letting them know they are missed, as opposed to no response at all or a more confrontive sounding text saying, *"Why aren't you here?"* Or it could be they need help navigating the dominator that continues to take over the group week after week or how to draw out the less talkative ones into the group conversation. All of these we cover in our training and leader's guide, but sometimes they still need some extra coaching.

- *It tells you if the person is in the right position.*

Everyone is not meant to be a leader of a group. If there is an attendance problem, it might be a leadership problem, or they could be out of position. For example, there are a number of reasons for spotty attendance. It could be work schedules, parent/teacher meetings, or sickness. But if they continue to not retain most people in their group from quarter to quarter, they may be out of position.

We had a couple that had been hosting groups for years. They were incredible people with great integrity, character, and complete servants. One of our staff thought we should consider making them hosts. We had some caution if it was a good fit. We were also concerned they may have a hard time telling you no because of how servant-oriented they are and willing to please. The response was they had grown and were ready to take on a new challenge. So the ask was made, and they launched into leading their group.

The first meeting was great because it's typical of a potluck/party-type situation. This couple was great at that and always had been. But little success after that. Not because of any character issues. They just weren't any good at taking the lead in the group or leading group discussions. After two painful quarters, we took them out of that position. They were relieved and even thanked us. And off they went, ready and willing to be back in the hosting role where they knew they belonged.

If someone is not having success, they're usually ready to get out of that position or may need someone to help them move on. Even when there is a character or moral issue, they are in conflict with leading, whether they cognitively know it or not. But know this: the last thing that we say to someone when needing to move them out of a position needs to be, "Here's what's next for you. You're not done!"

Every human is of great worth, created in God's image, and designed to serve. As pastors and leaders, we want to keep that vision alive in people, even if the reason you're pulling them out from that situation is due to a moral failure or a significant issue that's going on in their life that is creating a need for them to step back from leadership and focus on working through the issue at hand.

Our goal isn't to burn bridges so they don't come back but rather to create them to get help or find another role that fits them better. And if they find the help they need and grow themselves, the bridge can also offer an opportunity to return! I have repeatedly seen individuals go get the help they need and then come back over the bridge that was created for them to be effective in leading again and be as good, if not better than they were before.

Ways to create an information highway to get feedback:

Call me anytime!

You've already heard that we make ourselves available to our leaders 24/7 to help and that you don't need to worry about being overrun by calls from them. But if you do have a leader repeatedly contacting you on your private number, we need to care for them and find out what's going on. You may need to help them set a boundary for when they can randomly call you, or it may be related to a personal issue they're dealing with. But don't let an exception become your rule to shut down your availability with the fear of everyone doing the same.

We have never seen this become an issue, even at a church our size. Your leaders are not depending on you for their every move. They've got most of it covered. But they do need access to you quickly when the tough stuff comes. They don't typically need to spend time with you; they just need access to you when they are in a pinch.

Weekly Group Attendance

This is one of our most valuable processes to care for our leaders' leading groups and the members of their groups. Our leaders get an email the day after their group meeting to submit their attendance. Every Monday, our team has available to them an attendance summary of what their group's participation looks like. See an example of weekly group attendance in the Additional Resource Section (at the end of the book).

Some may initially think we're just checking up on them. And of course, there is some truth to that, but it's more about what we may need to do to help our leaders and how their groups are going. I've heard some say taking attendance is all about the numbers. And my answer quickly is, yes, it is. I hope everyone is. Every number represents an individual, and we care about those individuals.

Larry often talks about the need for clear budgeting in churches. He says it's important to know exactly what is being spent and to give precise donation receipts for tax purposes. If a church didn't do this, you'd probably worry about the leadership's responsibility, as it's crucial to track money accurately.

None of us would say we're all about the money. But why do we only track money and not our people? Doesn't that sound backwards? Isn't it irresponsible not to track what we care about the most? Proverbs 27:23 says, "Be sure you know the condition of your flocks." Why are we afraid to pay attention to our people? My guess is some are afraid of being seen as "big brother." Or is it because we're afraid of measuring our effectiveness?

I received a call a while back about a person who needed some help. For all our staff, our typical first response is, who knows them, and are they in a life group? In a matter of minutes, I was able to go to our database and see the last time they were in a life group. It was two years ago. I was hopeful I could bring support to them through the leader that they were in the group with or someone who knew them in the group. And that's exactly what happened. In a matter of two minutes, I was able to touch base with some key people from their group and create a game plan for care for this person. All because we took attendance in our life groups.

It also helps us with vetting volunteers for other ministries. If someone is signing up to be involved in another ministry and they're in a life group, which most of our people are, we are quickly able to get a reference on them.

This isn't big brother; it's caring for our people on a grand scale and in an incredibly timely way!

You may be asking, "Does someone's lack of attendance disqualify them?" You have to be careful when reading these reports and how we can make people become numbers instead of numbers being people. Missing attendance on this report doesn't tell us what is happening; it just tells us something out of the ordinary is occurring and may be worth asking a question. There could be a great reason someone may only come to half of their groups. They may be a first responder and their schedule swings from week to week. Or they had a crisis in their family.

As far as attendance in the group, it helps us see what's going on in the leader's mind also. If the leader is having 50% of their people show up every week, we realize the leader may be struggling, or at least we need to investigate to find out what's going on and to see if we can help. It may be because they have a group with a number of parents who have elementary-aged kids and they have repeated family obligations, or a number of people who have been sick, and the list goes on.

Again, it helps us investigate what's going on and truly care for our leaders and our people. That's why when new leaders sign up, we tell them how important the attendance process is; if we don't get it, we will annoy you until we do. And it's not about the numbers; it's because we care about them, the people God has given us to care for.

Feedback Forms

At the end of the quarter, every person in a group gets an email that has six simple questions about their group experience. For the most part, what we get back is affirmation to the leader and the host. Does everybody respond? No. This past couple of years, we've had a 30% response rate, which is statistically above-average. But it still seems low, and naturally, we wonder if it's worth the work if we're getting only 30%. And my answer is absolutely.

As I mentioned earlier, every healthy organization creates an avenue for feedback, which means we make sure we offer it, but we don't demand a response. I had a friend who was frustrated with his group for quite some time and struggled to figure out how to address it. Finally, he called me, and we talked through it. As we debriefed, I asked him what had kept him from calling sooner. Essentially, it came down to the fact that it was hard to make that call, even to me, a friend. I totally get that. I reminded him about using the feedback form as another way to let us know what's going on, and it was possibly a bit less intimidating.

At another time, he reached out to me via the feedback form to let me know about another tricky situation with his group member. He had found a comfortable way to communicate with us. *Success!* That's why we provide multiple layers of support. We can't make people respond, but we do make sure we invite them to if they'd like to.

Encourage to Give Significance

This is appreciation. Why is it important? Because we all need encouragement. Proverbs 3:27 says, "Do not withhold good from those to whom it is due when it is in your power to act." Rosabeth Moss Kanter, a professor at Harvard Business School and an Innovation and Change consultant, cuts right to the point regarding the power and importance of genuine encouragement: "Recognition is so easy to do and inexpensive that there is simply no excuse for not doing it." That is such an incredible statement. Encouragement is not complicated or expensive but needs to be real and specific. How do you affirm and encourage your leaders?

When I first became a youth pastor, one of my small group leaders, Jake, was a great leader. He had his squirrely freshman guys talking and interacting. He was doing a great job. And at the end of the night, I said, "Jake, you're doing an awesome job."

He said, "Thank you."

The next week, I saw him do the same thing. And I said again, "You're doing an awesome job."

He said, "Thank you."

And then the third week came, and I said again, "You're doing such an awesome job, Jake."

And this time, he said, "Awesome at what?"

What a great question. What I realized was that my compliment lacked specificity to give it meaning and value. In fact, it was borderline flattery, which is giving excessive praise essentially to be liked. Of course, I wanted Jake to be encouraged, but I could see my lack of specificity was now about me just being positive, saying what was affirming, and not showing that I really was taking the time to engage and appreciate what he was doing.

In fact, we can't truly encourage someone until we've observed and evaluated them. For example, when I meet with a group of pastors for training, I'm offering them I can't tell them they are all great pastors because the truth is, I have no idea if they are. However, I can say it's great to see you've taken the time away to invest in learning, that they're working on a new strategy to increase their effectiveness, etc.

As followers of Jesus, I do believe we can optimistically view people as we believe they are of great worth, created in God's image. Yet, all too often in the name of being a positive and optimistic follower of Jesus, we begin to look clueless and self-serving by giving compliments that have no foundation of observation. It's what I have done way too many times in my life, and it's what I like to call "blowing Christian smoke." Affirmation is vital for our souls, but we have to be specific about how or why we appreciate someone.

People need to be affirmed and recognized for what they have accomplished. To do this, we create appreciation and connection moments and events for our leaders throughout the year that tell them we're here, we care, and appreciate you.

Five Connects a Week. Have you ever received a short, unexpected text or voicemail from a friend who's just checking in to say hi to let you know they're thinking about you or remember something you have going on? It's almost always appreciated because it tells you what matters to them. That's how we would define a "connect." It's a text, email, note, phone call, coffee, meal, with one leader to encourage them. The goal is to simply say, "I'm thinking about you," when they don't expect it and don't want anything in return. This is our weekly goal for us as staff when it comes to reaching out to our leaders. Over a period of five weeks, you'll have made connections with twenty-five different leaders.

What I've also noticed over the years is that those who do this most consistently with their leaders often receive more leader referrals of potential leaders. I believe this is a result of how this approach helps build a genuine connection, going beyond just being something they are doing for the church or a role we need to fill.

Leadership gatherings. We never want to miss telling our leaders how much we appreciate them whenever we meet. It's always part of our gatherings. The thanks we receive from them by providing childcare and a meal tells us we also help fill their affirmation bucket.

Weekly Attendance follow-up. Each week, look at their attendance. Our response to that is not focused on evaluation but rather on how we can come alongside and affirm them, maximizing the ministry opportunity they are in.

Christmas Cards and Handwritten "Thank You" Notes. Every year, we send out Christmas cards, and not just digitally, actual mailed Christmas cards that have pictures of us with our families because we want to end up on their refrigerator somewhere where they can see us. We want their kids to see our picture in their house. It's a small act that says, "We're here. And your family matters to us."

At the end of every year, we also give handwritten "thank you" notes to all of our leaders and hosts. Studies abound on the difference a written note makes. What's interesting is we hear stories of those notes being posted on a bulletin board or somewhere for the individual. Giving them another reminder that they are appreciated and we're thankful for who they are and what they do. In this digital age, it is important we don't miss the value of a handwritten note.

Implementing the Four Es into Your Model

One of the questions I'm asked about the Four Es is which one is most important. The answer is probably the one you do the least. The concentric circles below show how they are dependent upon each other.

NEXT STEPS STRATEGY: What do we need to need to start, stop, tweak, or keep?

Empower through Vision: When and how are you creating vision for connection and the importance of groups to your church as a whole? When and how do you cast vision for your group leaders?

Equip for Ministry: What are those key tools that you need to offer your leaders and people in the groups to have successful meetings and build friendships centered on Christ?

Evaluate for Success: Are you allowing feedback on how they're doing and you? Are they hearing feedback from the people in their groups?

Encourage to Give Significance: How and when are you specifically affirming your group leaders?

Final Questions:

- How do the 4 E's show up on your calendar?
- What are you good at? What needs improvement?
- How do you put these four into practice?

CHAPTER 5

Connect Someone

"Alone, we can do so little; together, we can do so much"
- Helen Keller

"So they devoted themselves to the Apostles' teaching and the fellowship and the breaking and bread and the prayer." - Acts 2:42

They Googled a nearby coffee shop with a good outdoor space. They needed a place to grab a cup of coffee and let their two young boys run around while they had a conversation. North Coast Coffee Shop came up, so out the door they headed. Upon arriving, they realized the coffee shop was on our church campus. Not quite what they expected, but they decided to stay.

The conversation they were having was too important to put off. They were working out the logistics of how to file for a divorce and what that would mean for their young family. After getting their coffee, they saw a flier for Life Groups—sign-ups were starting that week.

After a short talk and possibly some tears, they decided to attend a church service and possibly look into this Life Groups thing. They knew their isolation wasn't good, but they hadn't been sure what to do about it. They began to attend regularly and got connected with a great group. This story was years ago, but flashing forward to today, they are happily married, with one more kid in the mix, too! They had a plan, but God had a better plan.

I am confident you've encountered some miraculous stories as well. We know the power of connection is real! We're designed for it, and when it's lacking, we're not at our best. But if it's our greatest need, then why aren't more people joining our groups? Great question. Let's dive into it.

How Will They Know?

If I went to your church three weekends in a row, what would I say is important? Worship? Teaching? Snacks? Jesus? People? Media? Children's Ministry? Gifts for visitors? How about six weeks in a row? Would it change? How long would it take for me to hear that connection with others is important? Would there be any clarity on how it happens besides going to the visitor information booth? How often would I hear real examples of how people are connected in your church?

One of the questions we get asked often is how many sermons are given about groups and the importance of connection to get people to sign up for a group. My answer?—most of them. Over the 33 years I've been at North Coast, I've only heard five or six messages exclusively on the importance of groups and relationships, but hundreds of sermons where this concept is dripped in. Whatever is important to us should be easily heard and found out beyond an announcement or promotion for an event.

Larry coined this "the drip method." Jesus and the connection in groups are the two biggest messages we want to get out there. It's no surprise Jesus is a recurring theme, but many are surprised groups are, too. I had a pastor visit one time after I mentioned this to him. He said he heard groups mentioned seven times in a non-group-focused sermon. Life groups will get dripped in weekend messages with comments like this:

"You know, when you're out with your friends in your life group and..."

"I was with my friends in my life group, and someone said..."

"We were laughing and talking about this at life group and..."

We want our language to communicate an assumption. The language isn't, *Are you in a group?* It's, *Who's group are you in?* And if we haven't heard life groups mentioned for three weekends in a row, as I mentioned earlier, I have the green light to remind our teaching pastor about it. There have only been a couple of times over the years I've had to do that.

We're able to do this because it's vital to our leadership team. Larry started this years ago when we launched our groups ministry. And now, with Chris Brown at the helm for the past five years, it remains the same!

Here's something many don't know about when we hired Chris. Chris has a dynamic storytelling teaching gift. He can make the stories of the Bible come alive, and people want to hear it. Yet, Larry made it clear to Chris that even if his teaching gift reached thousands more, but we didn't maintain the same percentage in groups, his hire would be considered a failure. That's how important connection and groups are to us! The point is, community is not seen as secondary to Bible study—the two go hand in hand. We believe you can't talk about one without the other. That's why you'll also rarely miss a week hearing about our Life Groups at North Coast. It's a significant marker of spiritual health, and we want to make sure it's abundantly clear!

The priority from our teaching and leadership team to get people in groups is foundational to our level of success. Without it, we would not be where we are. Every organization is a reflection of its leadership. If you're wondering if your team will take the next steps, know that it is a process and must be strategic. Chapter 8 will help you build a strategic plan for your church to move in that direction.

Who Are Your Groups For?

The people in your church care about what you care about. As you drip in the story of connection and groups, you also want to be clear on who your groups are for and their purpose. How you talk about them matters. If you talk about groups being for those who want to get serious about Bible study and really dig in, then you'll only get the most serious and committed. If you focus too much on just meeting friends, then it becomes just another social gathering.

Our groups are about building friendships that encourage and support you as you follow Jesus. It's why we changed the name of our groups from "Growth Groups" to "Life Groups." It seemed to describe more easily what our groups were about, doing life together. We designed our system to encourage the last 25% of the congregation to get in a group. If your system is designed to appeal to the most committed to join a group, only the most committed will join. If it's designed to get the least committed to join, the others will follow.

Our hope is to help everyone, no matter what place you're at in your faith, to get connected in relationships that are going to help you understand who Jesus is, how to follow him, and find people to do life with.

Is It Doable?

Provide a doable time commitment and an escape clause. The two questions almost always asked before someone joins a group are: "How long is the commitment?" and "What if I end up in a group that isn't a good fit?" One of the genius things that caught my attention over 30 years ago when I came to North Coast and first joined a life group was that the commitment was only ten weeks. If I didn't think it was a good fit those first few weeks, I could see if there was a better one to join. After that ten weeks, I could stay in the same group, try a new group, or drop out if my schedule is going crazy without feeling like I'm someone lacking commitment.

In the past, my experience had been that group commitments were either simply a matter of showing up when you can or an almost indefinite commitment lasting nine months or a full year. Without commitment, trust and care cannot be built. However, the long-term commitment was intended only for the fully committed, which is not our target group. Finally, someone was offering a manageable commitment.

The 10-week quarter works well because it typically takes three weeks just to get a rhythm going for a group and how it works. We essentially offer three 10-week quarters: fall, winter, and spring, and take the summer off. Groups are welcome to meet during the summer but never expected. Some do, but most don't. The breaks have offered a welcomed respite for everyone between quarters throughout the year.

Surprisingly, a longer summer break has been especially important for leaders and hosts, giving them needed downtime and allowing them to be ready to go again in the fall. We've had leaders at the end of the spring thinking they are going to take the next year off. But because the summer gave them the break they needed, they were ready to lead again in the fall. We believe this is one of the reasons we've been able to have strong retention of leadership year after year.

We offer sign ups three times a year at the beginning of each quarter. This creates an expectant urgency and momentum to get signed up. We sign up only new people to the group, with existing members remaining in the group from quarter to quarter. (See diagram below.)

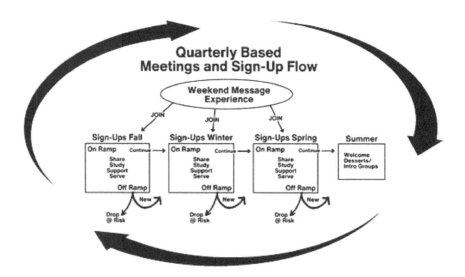

Once the quarter starts, we consider our groups as closed. This is important in the process of building safety and trust within the group. The pushback on this is, what if someone shows up at your church and wants to join a group? Are you going to make them wait that long to get a group? Maybe.

First, it's extremely rare that someone is going to show up at your church and choose to make a 10-week commitment to a group knowing very little about your church or groups. In our experience, the majority of those that do this, rarely show up to the group. Most people who sign up for a group after attending services for at least a month or more will know about upcoming sign-up opportunities and will be somewhat aware of how the groups go. In the rare case it does happen that someone has a high sense of urgency or is "crisis-like" about joining a group immediately, it's likely they are in need of pastoral care rather than group care. A pastor spending some extra on the phone or even meeting them in person can make all the difference.

Second, we do allow people to join groups up to 2 to 3 weeks after signups have ended and the group has started because we realize some people may have been gone on the weekends signups were offered. But again, the number of people who do this is small, largely because people are aware of when life group sign-ups will be since we talk about it and advertise it so much.

Also, sign-ups online are extremely easy and are now the primary way people sign up for groups. Our current lead pastor, Chris Brown and his wife, also have ""Welcome Desserts" every quarter for our new attendees. This is another way they can connect with others while they wait to get into a life group. Most people asking to sign up mid quarter are fine with waiting a few weeks for our next welcome desert or sign up season for groups. With all that said, we do make exceptions and do on occasion place people in groups outside of the typical sign up time. It's just not the norm. And we don't want to change our process because of an exception, rather we will just make the exception when needed.

The feeling of safety in our groups is very important to us. The reason I spend so much time on this is because I think we forget the safety needed in groups for people to build relationships and be able to be real about their life's difficulties and struggles. And consistency creates safety. We all too often look at the exception and then decide to make it a norm, not realizing the much larger consequence.

Retention and Size

The ideal size for a group is 12-14 people. Once you get to 16 people, there are too many people to be able to really hear from everyone, every time, which is our goal. People start to feel like they are not needed in the group, and overall attendance drops. And in fact, people are even happy that a few people didn't show! It gives you the opportunity for better conversation. The value and priority to attend drops when you realize you may be engaged. But if you know you are needed, that your contribution is important and will be missed, you make a much greater effort to be there.

Here is what we go by—10 registrations in a group means the group is a "go," 8 is an "I don't know," and 6 is an "I don't think so." People typically connect in smaller groups of 3 to 4 within a group which is why 12 to 14 is such a sweet spot. It gives someone multiple options of people to connect with while still keeping the energy of critical mass. 10 people in a group still gives you that. 8 in a group depends on everyone rarely missing to keep critical mass. If suddenly a few don't, there's a loss of momentum.

We do have leaders ask for their group to be 16 or more because the number of people showing up keeps dropping below 8, even though they have 12 to 14 signed up. This is a warning sign that something may be going on in the group that needs some attention. People often think enthusiasm will keep everyone in the group. That will work for a short time, but not over the long haul. Engagement is why people stay in a group, even if they may look like they don't want to.

Rhythm of Groups and Relationships

The 10 weeks also works great for the rhythm of relationships. We start with a fun night with typically a meal together and get-to-know-you questions and set the sights for the quarter (see for more details – Setting Your Groups up for Success in Chapter 6). Then at some point in the quarter, we also asked the groups to have a social together. Breaking the routine of the meeting to do something fun creates a new kind of energy and connection for the group. They typically use their regular meeting time for this since it already works for their schedules. They also have the option to do a service project during any of the quarters. We end each quarter with a celebration of how God has worked, reflecting and typically taking communion together. And then confirming who is returning and who is staying in the group so they are ready for the next quarter at that last meeting.

Our questions for groups also have a rhythm to them. Their depth and focus start lighter in the beginning and progress as the group builds its trust week to week. It's truly the rhythm of a relationship.

The Escape Clause

The escape clause is also important and is made clear during our sign-up weeks at North Coast. One of the biggest fears we hear from people when joining a group is what if they get in one they don't like and are afraid they can't get out. Everyone deals with that. We have fun with this idea as we communicate it on all our weekend sign ups yet remain purposeful in letting them know they don't have to worry about getting stuck.

We typically say something like this, "We realize that you might be worried about getting in a group with a bunch of strange people. However, they might think you're a strange person! Seriously, we do understand that fear. We know good people don't always connect. We are so committed to relationships and a good fit; we want to do all we can to help you with that. And if during the first three weeks you find yourself in a group that doesn't seem like a good fit, please let us know, and we'll do all we can to find you a group that works for you."

It's not often that people take us up on this, but our honesty about it helps build a sense of trust and authenticity with our people regarding our groups and our commitment to them.

We also tell people it may take trying a few different groups over time to find the best fit. It gives them opportunities and options. Everyone wants opportunities and options, and it lowers the expectation of everything being close to perfect in the beginning. After a few weeks, most stick with their group for the 10-week commitment.

Understand the Competition

One of the reasons people may not sign up for your groups is that the competition for their time at your church is too great. One of my primary roles in my job is to keep the Life Group banner high. For example, we don't have sign-ups for many other things around the signup season for groups. We know people will typically only give their church two time slots a week.

I mentioned earlier that at North Coast we choose to schedule little if any ministry activities during the week. Years ago, we decided that our children's ministry (up to 5th grade) would only be offered during weekend services. (The exception to this is our junior high, high school, and young adult ministries. However, in order for someone to volunteer in these student ministries, we ask that they are also in a life group). That said, I'm constantly amazed by what our children's ministry staff is doing on the weekends. As for volunteers, they are only asked to serve at one service time, two weekends per month. This allows them to still attend a weekend service themselves at least twice a month and keeps them fresh for leading. This is also so they are available to join a life group for a weekly commitment and/or lead or host a life group.

We believe the most important thing to help kids follow Jesus is that their parents have growing relationships with Jesus and others. But if parents' time is too monopolized by serving in weekend and midweek ministry, children's or otherwise, they have less time to build the relationships their kids need to witness. Children will see their parents involved in ministry but not necessarily building Christ-centered relationships.

Now, even though we don't hold midweek children's ministry activities, it's still one of the most important ministries in our church. Having thriving and attractive children's programs is also a surprisingly successful form of outreach for us. Families are coming to North Coast because of it. I've heard variations of this story too many times to count: A kid invites their friend to church, and they go. When they return, the friend's parents are surprised to hear that he loved it and wants to go with their friend again. The parents agree because they figure it's a good place for their kid to be. After a few weekends of their kid repeatedly coming home excited about their church experience, the parents are befuddled—*how is it that my kid actually likes going to church?* They often become curious and begin to attend themselves. And this is all happening without having a midweek children's ministry.

We do the same for many of our other ministries that require volunteers. For our worship teams - no practice during the week. Only before the service. This is intentional because we want our people in groups. We want them to be part of a community that can actually do life with them.

Here's a little more about why we want as little as possible competing against our people doing church in circles, not just rows or serving in other ministries. Let's be honest. Even with the best intentions, most married couples don't pray together, study the Bible together, or talk about sermons they just heard and figure out how to apply them to their lives. And this is true for many people in most of their relationships, not just between couples. But it's not typically because people don't want to do these things. So why don't they? The answer is the same reason we all, church staff and pastors included, don't always invest in our spiritual lives in the way we'd like to. We get distracted, busy, forget, or don't really have a set space in our life where it can happen. But what happens when a couple joins a life group? They are suddenly doing all these things together as a couple, individually and with others too!

Let's return to the verse discussed earlier, "bad company corrupts good morals" (1 Corinthians 15:33). While the original audience this verse was intended to reach was adults, we know the principle does apply to our children as well. As parents, we know how formidable those teen years are, and like us, their friends can make a significant difference in their lives and faith. Yet, telling our kids about the importance of Christian friends won't have near the impact if we're not modeling those kinds of relationships ourselves. If we want kids to appreciate the importance of building good Christian friendships, parents have to be doing it too. They can talk about it, but it's just words unless they're doing it. As a church, we want to create as little competition for their time to make that happen.

Options and Simplicity

Provide a clear and simple way to sign up that offers multiple on-demand group options on various days and locations. This allows them to self-select their group of choice. We have three ways people can sign up during the times of year when we offer sign-ups: online, at a weekend service, or by calling the church office during the week. The bio information that includes interests, hobbies, and pictures of the leader and host is important because it helps people find the kind of people they want to be in a group with. They often think location first when looking for a group, but they usually choose people most like themselves over driving distance.

Provide Groups in Various Neighborhoods in the Community of Your Church Campus

If groups are important, they need to be accessible in a variety of locations on a variety of days and you have to offer more openings than the number of people that you think will sign up. To illustrate this, we use the visual of having "enough coats on the rack." Imagine seeing the coat that you've been wanting is finally for sale. You rush to the store and see it in all of its glory at an incredible price. You get so excited! As you get closer to the rack however, you discover there is only one size available, and that one size definitely doesn't fit you. You are disappointed of course, but maybe you feel like you were just too late. A few months later, another sale happens. You rush back to the store with the same result again. No coats that fit you and the colors available were not as advertised. The third time the coats get released, you have no rush in going to the store to check availability. In fact you may even avoid going to the store all together. You know it's just hype, and there is little authentic effort in trying to offer the customer what they need. You've lost hope and are now discouraged because what they offer just will not fit.

If we say "life groups are the key to building relationships, please join one" - but we don't make them accessible, we are sending a similar mixed message of "not having enough coats on the rack." Having ample availability is necessary when we believe that groups are a big deal and that a high majority of people should be involved in one. In fact, filling all of our groups is actually a failure. Because just like the analogy of having enough coats on the rack, you have to have more openings in groups than the number expected to sign up. When we cancel some groups because they didn't fill it is actually a success. It indicates we had plenty of openings in a group or had "enough coats on the rack" for the customer to have doable choices.

To ensure we are doing this, we plan for an extra 10-15% of openings beyond our projected sign ups. For example if we think we're going to have 100 people sign up, then we would then need 110 to 115 open seats at various locations and days. We also want to watch for what we call a "false positive" that makes it look like we have more openings than we really have. Examples of false positives would be offering groups at times or locations that aren't really feasible for your community. It looks like you have open seats, but they're not realistic options. We have found in our community that most people sign up for groups on Wednesday and Thursday evenings, so now the majority of our options are on those days. If we offer three groups on a Monday night, chances are that only one will fill. We also know that it is difficult to fill a group if it is offered more than 20 minutes from our campus. In each of those examples of false positives, it looks like we have enough openings, but they aren't realistic. If groups are for everyone, they need to be known for being available and accessible to everyone.

Stage of Life vs. Location

Think twice about grouping people together geographically. One of the other keys is when they sign up; we don't put the exact location and or address, just a general location. What we have found is that people stick longer when they find people like themselves to join a group. That's why the descriptions in the bios are important for people finding a group.

But it's not usually where they start. They typically start with location because that is their initial highest priority. What we have found is good friends are worth driving to. When we started our groups model years ago, all our groups were labeled as general, in other words, available for all ages and stages. That was important because it gave people the most options to join a group.

It's also what we do when we launch a new campus with thirty groups or less. We don't want to label them young families or parents of teens groups even though there is an urge to because of the attractional nature of offering those kinds of groups. Yet, when a campus has fewer than 30 groups, it lacks the critical mass needed to fill those kinds of groups. Plus, we've found keeping the lines fuzzy for who can join a group essential because at some point, most families don't fit into one category. One family can have an elementary-aged child and another away at college.

The fuzzy lines allow them to have options. Describing the leaders and hosts in the bio, along with their interests, is a great move toward helping people find a good fit for themselves. We found this out years ago when we needed to divide the load of groups among multiple staff. The question was whether we should divide ourselves by station of life or by geographic location to the church. We had about 120 groups, all considered general. As we looked, to our surprise, the majority had already self-selected the stage of life over geographic location – we already had multiple parents of teens, young families, and even empty nest groups choosing stage of life over location. They confirmed it—good friends are worth driving to.

> **Welcoming in New People—Don't Give Them the Address to Where They Meet!**
>
> Another reason we don't give out the addresses is that it forces the leaders to ensure they send out that expectant welcoming call for the first meeting. This way, newcomers are welcomed and given directions. We also make the first meeting a food and, for the most part, an upbeat and fun night. We still get serious, but that food element, again, is something that attracts people to attend that first meeting.
>
> Additionally, if it works in your context to have a potluck where everyone contributes to that first meal, any new person will instantly be contributing to that first meeting and be responsible for helping make it a good one. Please note that as you think through this strategy, it takes time to work out the details.
>
> One of our suggestions is to practice this model with a few groups to help refine your processes.

NEXT STEPS STRATEGY: What do we need to start, stop, tweak, or keep?

On a scale of one to five, with one being low to never and five being weekly, how often do weekend attendees hear about connection during service?

Does the design of your groups attract and appeal to those you want in groups? (Think through group location and availability, language that is used to promote groups, and the time commitment of groups).

What is the rhythm of groups? Does it include a defined start with an inviting welcome and clear direction, a build up of questions as the weeks progress, and socials or service projects? How and when do groups end?

What competes with groups, and does that lessen the value of being in a group? What other announcements or program sign-ups are going on during the group sign-up season?

CHAPTER 6

Support Someone

"All leaders of equal value, but all don't need equal attention. Therefore, encourage one another and build one another up just as you are doing." - 1 Thessalonians 5:11

What support do you need to offer your leaders? It's one of the big questions out there and continually discussed. How do you know what's happening in their groups and if they are getting the encouragement, accountability, and support they need? The answer I often hear is to provide a coaching system. Our approach is a bit different.

Here's our story.

Years ago, before I moved into the group role, we created our L5 coaching system, where one life group leader coaches five other life group leaders. The org chart looked fantastic. We had some great coaching retreats and meetings. I was a youth pastor then and led one of our adult groups. I was invited to join the coaches even though I wasn't in a coaching role. Whenever I attended the retreats and meetings, I found them worth my time as they built into my leadership and friendships with other leaders. I also remember being a bit surprised that never more than half of the coaches showed up.

Because I was a small group leader, I was assigned a coach. We never actually had a meeting. I didn't need one. I recall one afternoon, my L5 coach just happened to be by our staff offices. He peeked into my office and asked me if we needed to meet for a coaching session. I really didn't. We talked for a few minutes, and that was it. I would venture to say that we both left that encounter, realizing that not everyone needs a coach.

Fast forward seven years later, when I took over our life group ministry. Our L5 coaching system had continued to decline and was now sputtering along, barely alive. In my new role, I was rubbing shoulders with small group pastors from other churches. The overwhelming consensus was that having a coaching system in place for small group leaders was important for the success of the groups. Being new in my role and hearing about the importance of coaches, I was committed to rolling up my sleeves and making it happen successfully!

My plan was to revamp how we were going about it and find a way to make it work. I brought in 12 of our top long-term group leaders to become coaches. They were excited they had been asked, yet right from the beginning, they had doubts about this model. What came up very quickly with these 12 veteran leaders was that they unanimously believed that not everybody needs a coach. So they came up with an idea, a different system of support: a "Wingman" approach, available if needed. We created a few purposeful touchpoints to offer throughout the year and launched our new system.

A year went by, and we sat down to reassess, checking in to see how many connections happened. It was well below 50%. Not the success we had hoped for, and not because my select 12 didn't give it a valiant effort. So, we buckled up and tried to do better the next year.

Three years later, the Wingman's effectiveness still didn't result in the success we had hoped it would. The pattern was clear. However, everything else was going great in our groups ministry. Groups were going well. We were recruiting new leaders. We were retaining leadership. We were effectively dealing with problems. We were aware of what was going on.

With some reluctance, the idea came up: *What if we canceled our Wingman coaching system?* But that didn't seem quite right. Our groups are too important to allow the "crashing and burning" of our leaders due to a lack of support! This was a risk, for sure. We took the leap of faith and went for it! And here's what happened—nothing. All of the successful elements of our small groups ministry continued to flow well, just as they had before. We found out we weren't failing; we were, in fact, succeeding. As we dug in some more, here's what we found as to why.

What We've Learned About Offering Our Leaders Support

Too often, we treat our leaders like followers, meaning we fall into the trap of thinking they need more than they do and then overwork trying to provide something they won't use. That's what was happening with our coaching system. What we were overlooking was the fact that the people we were recruiting to lead and host our groups were in the top 20%. They are leader types, which lends itself to being self-feeders. They initiate more than most.

Of course, the level of this varies in speed and how it looks, but remember, they are all committed "to being successful enough," and they stepped up to lead and care for others. They were also recommended because someone saw that they take initiative in doing the right thing and serving others. It's the Pareto principle, where 20% of the people accomplish 80% of the results. It's why they are in the role they are in.

The need for assigning a coach wasn't high because they were initiators who could get help themselves and were often good with people and problem-solving. But they do need access to help when and if they need it. That's why quick and easy access to us is so important, but also, again, why we don't get overrun with calls. We trust our leaders to be doing what we hope they are doing and are able to give them the support and attention they need on a large scale without a typical coaching system.

As we took a closer look, we found five reasons why things were going so well without a coaching system:

1. *Referral-Based Recruiting*: This is one of the key reasons we can trust our leaders, and we believe they will most often have good judgment when it comes to leading their group and getting help when they need it. People of reputation have recommended them. There is a referral from the person who recommended them. The entire staff or lead team saw no concern when a "flag check" was emailed. And they were met with personally by you, heard their story, and believed in their character. We are going to trust their character to make good decisions until we hear otherwise.

2. *Shared Leadership and the Group Environment*: Our shared leadership model offers encouragement, sharing the load, and accountability. We have both a leader couple and a host couple. They create a built-in support system. The group itself creates an atmosphere of encouragement and accountability. This is happening every week. We don't want to underestimate that.

3. *Weekly Attendance*: Attendance and retention in the group is one of our best indicators of how the connection in the group is going and how the leader is doing. To be clear, attendance doesn't tell us exactly what is happening; rather, it is an indicator if something is happening out of the ordinary and if investigation is needed. If attendance is down or significantly fluctuating, we know the leadership may need some extra attention and encouragement.

4. *Training Rhythm and Real-Time Resources*: Our training rhythm provides them with the tools, training, and expectations to know what success is and how to accomplish it.

5. *Staff Access and Availability*: All of our group leaders have full-time 24/7 access and availability to contact us as staff when they need some extra help, another perspective, or encouragement. We call it on-demand coaching. And as mentioned earlier, we are not overrun with calls because most leaders know how to deal with most issues.

Another question that follows is, if there are no coaches, then do you ever expect staff to meet with leaders one-on-one? And how would they do that with such limited time? Don't they need at least some of that? It's a great question. The only time we require a one on one meeting is when we interview them to become a leader. This goes back to the same reasons why we don't need to provide them with an ongoing personal coaching system. They are leaders and typically already have a support system around them or will once they are in a shared leadership partnership in their group.

Our leader's priority isn't time with us; it's accessibility when they have a need. Of course, if you're a new or smaller ministry and have just a few leaders, you would naturally be able to spend more one-on-one time with them because your options for friends are smaller at your church. But again, they may not need that one-on-one time with you because they already have it somewhere else. Yet, no matter the size, they need to know we're available. And just because we tell them, they still may not believe it.

Here's how we make sure they believe it. Every week, when we look over their attendance, which we set aside to do on Mondays, we talk about the importance of one "Connect" with five different leaders every week. What is a "Connect?"? It's a text, email, note, phone call, a coffee, meal, with one leader to encourage them and ask nothing from them. The goal is to simply say I'm thinking about you when they don't expect it and not wanting anything in return.

So, over a period of five weeks, we'll have made a connection with twenty-five different leaders that tells them you are thinking about them and you're available. It has nothing to do with anything you want from them. It only has to do with that either you're praying for them, something has reminded you of them, been reminded about in their conversation, or something that they're doing; it's something that says I'm thinking about you today. And it shouts, *I'm here, available, and accessible when you need me.* All of this can be accomplished in only 30 to 60 minutes a week. It's so simple to do; it seems like there's no excuse for not doing it.

Even though we expect our staff to meet with each leader one-on-one, we do expect them to ask, "Is there anyone that specifically needs my attention?" This is usually easily tuned into by looking at their group attendance each week to see if there are notes from the leader or attendance changes. The principle that drives us here is that all leaders are of equal value, but all don't need equal attention. The barometer offered by attendance, experience, and any takeaways from our initial interactions helps us know where and when to turn up our attention.

Train Your Small Group Leaders to Deal with Just About Anything

Power of Asking Questions and Being Slow to Give Advice

We want to train your leaders on how to deal with most issues that come up. I realize this sounds like a mammoth task. But again, the group leader's job is not to solve people's problems; it's to ask questions to find out what resources they need. We came up with this years ago, emphasizing the importance of question-asking, which I think we understand is key in leading groups.

One of the great privileges of leading small groups is having the opportunity to help someone work through a challenging life issue and help them grow as a result. Yet, the fear of dealing with these issues can cause a leader to never sign up to lead, quit, or do all they can to remain on the surface to avoid any messes. It's also what can cause a well-intentioned leader to become a "Bible answer assault person," quoting Bible verses at someone hoping to fix the problem, unaware of how to come alongside and help (Galatians 6:1-2).

To help our leaders embrace the tough stuff and create an environment for growth, we'd like them to ask these four simple questions and then if needed reach out to us for any additional assistance or resources.

The Four Questions

Imagine someone approaches and needs help with an issue they are dealing with. It could be depression, a financial problem, pornography, a health concern, gender confusion, a marital issue, a work conflict, etc. As a leader, we often think we need to come up with an answer and fix it. We believe that asking the four questions below before we try to solve anything will give a simple yet profound understanding of how to help this person and what resources you may be able to help them access to deal with the issue. These are essential to knowing how to give advice if asked.

1. *How long has this been going on?* (Duration of the issue): This question offers timely context to the potential depth of the issue. Understanding whether the issue has existed for days, weeks, months, or years is essential in assessing the level of help they may need and who, if anyone, needs to be involved. It also helps you to assess if this is an urgent situation or if it's been going on for a while. A leader's response may be different depending on the findings of this answer. Also, by asking this question, it communicates your willingness to listen. Being heard is sometimes all people need to be motivated to move forward because they realize they have an advocate. It empowers you to accurately empathize with them.

2. *Who else knows?* (Involvement of others): Finding out if you're the only person they have ever told reveals their level of vulnerability with you on the issue, if they are operating in isolation on this issue, and the kind of support and influence they have. Finding out who they gather around them for support gives you insight into their current state.

3. *What advice or counsel have you already received?* (Level and quality of input so far): Just because someone has told others about their issue doesn't mean they have sought counsel on how to overcome it or are motivated to start dealing with it. They may only want others to sympathize with their difficulty. Who they've received advice from can make the difference. A couple who comes to you after seeing four different counselors over the past five years is much different than a couple who is sharing something with you that they are dealing with for the very first time. Also, finding out if there is any input they received that they disagree with can tell you a lot about how they are processing what they hear.

4. *What would you like to do from here?* (Game plan from this point forward): This question keeps them empowered in a difficult situation and helps you find out their motivation for coming to you and whether they are ready to move forward. You can only move forward with them if they are willing. Here again, we have to be careful of giving unsolicited advice. If they don't know, you can ask if they'd like your feedback or if you can check on or suggest any options or resources. This helps open the door for them to receive input. Offering options is important to keep them empowered, able to make decisions, and not feel helpless.

We have found these four questions to be easy and powerful for any leader to obtain the facts and context they need to provide assistance. They usually make finding the next steps and necessary resources relatively straightforward when dealing with the situation. If a leader requires additional support or information, they can always contact us for further assistance. We don't expect our leaders to be experts in handling these issues; instead, we encourage them to be individuals who care for those whom God has brought to them, helping them navigate the challenges they encounter.

Confidentiality Reminder –You never know what someone is going to tell you. That's why we won't promise confidentiality. More on how we graciously respond to that request in the Additional Resource Section.

Three Kinds of Issues Will Come up That All Require Different Kinds of Responses

1. *There are life crisis issues.* They've lost a job, there's been an accident, they have cancer, their house is flooded, whatever it is, this is a general life crisis occurring.

2. *There are sin issues* that we need to engage people in and to talk with. Galatians 6:1 and Matthew 18 are our guides here. This is not about making accusations but coming alongside and asking questions as to what's behind the decisions that brought about the action and how they're processing this. Again, our availability on the front end to help coach and assist is important.

3. *There are group dynamic issues.* Group dynamic issues, whether they are personality issues or behavioral (dominator, not showing respect, etc.) and how they're interacting with the people, are oftentimes the most difficult to deal with because they look to be personality-driven and not morally based or sinful. This next statement I'm going to make is vital that you tune into. And chances are it's going to surprise you because it's the most subtle yet number one destroyer of groups to build the authentic connection people need. It's dealing with dominators (also known as overtalkers)! We've already covered that

our goal or task for a great meeting is to hear from everyone every time you meet. So when that's not happening, we have to ask why.

Most commonly, it is because there is a dominator or "overtalker" in the group. That helps begin to address that issue. It's a key element of our new leader training. We tell our leaders that most groups have one, and if you don't know who it is, it could be you!

Personality issues are another piece. Keep in mind, it is a privilege to be in a group, not a right. There is a standard of social decorum that must be met to remain in the groups. For groups to be effective, they must feel safe. Without the feeling of safety, there will be little meaningful conversation. In fact, people will stop coming. Though this is a necessary standard, it's not hard to obtain. It's actually quite simple. When someone else is talking, show respect, even if the thought or idea is different from your own. As the life group leader, it's your responsibility to ensure this type of safe environment. It's what turns acquaintances into friends. The pattern of every group I've been a part of starts with strangers and eventually emerges into committed, caring connections. Trust and safety are the binding ingredients.

Help your leaders differentiate between the three kinds of challenges in their group and how you can offer support

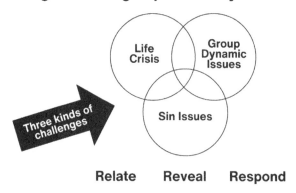

Relate   Reveal   Respond

Hearing From Everyone

As mentioned earlier, a key value of our Life Group model is that we want everyone in the group to have the opportunity to participate every time they meet. This counterintuitive concept may seem to contradict the intrinsic value of wanting everyone to feel safe. Can they both go together? We believe they not only can but that this duo is part of the magic sauce for the growth and strength of our groups.

People feel valued and safe when they can express themselves, knowing that both their words and their identity matter. Naturally, everyone has different comfort levels when it comes to sharing, and we respect those boundaries. Yet, by establishing a standard that we want to hear from every participant during the meeting, we encourage many to voice their thoughts when they might not have otherwise.

Group Dynamics With Dominators

We want everyone to be able to talk. We coach leaders to say, "Hey, we appreciate that you have things to say, but when you are talking for a long time or taking over, that's no longer giving other people the chance to participate, and they are tuning you out. We know you want to be tuned in to and to be listened to. I want to help you be heard well."

We have had conversations with multiple people as adults, and they have come back and said, "Thank you. No one has ever talked to me about this." Because here's what's interesting: typically, the Dominator is dealing with some isolation issues. They are talking (or thinking about talking) so much that they have no opportunity to connect and move toward others by listening, and others aren't going to move toward them because they know they won't be heard. A key element to understand is that relational growth can result in spiritual growth.

When a Leader Needs More Support

There are three ways we support our leaders when they encounter a challenging issue and are uncertain about the next steps. First, we begin by asking them the Four Questions mentioned earlier. This helps us gain context to determine how to provide support and allocate the necessary resources. Once those questions are answered, we transition to what we term the "You go, we go, I go" approach.

You Go: We start by talking through the issue with the leader, give them support on how to proceed, and agree on a good way to handle it. If the leader feels comfortable taking it from there, we empower them to proceed. We follow up to see how it went and how else we can help.

We Go: This step is taken when the leader isn't at the point where they believe they can deal with the situation on their own and need some direct assistance. Then it's a "we go." It can also be the next step when the leader has attempted to remedy the situation on their own, with our support, and more action is needed. We go together with them to engage in the issue.

I Go: The third option is typically a high-level issue where a pastor needs to deal directly with the individual for whom the concern was raised. Most leaders can effectively deal with most issues once they have the needed support. "Pastor-only" issues are quite rare. However, if this is an issue that is beyond your leader's reach or scope, it's important, as the pastor, to take the helm.

It's not unusual that leaders, at times, want the pastor to intervene right away, and understandably so. The truth is, sometimes situations are messy, and directly addressing an issue can be quite uncomfortable and scary. However, bringing your leaders into that journey can be very growing for them as a leader and equip them even better for future conversations.

Once your leaders are trained, they still need to know how to set their group up for success. It starts with the first meeting. The first meeting starts with a lot of fun and mingling, but also an important time to set the direction for the group and how to maximize their time together. If they don't, they'll have a much harder time directing their group and addressing any issues. And every group will have issues.

Setting Your Groups Up for Success

After your leaders are trained, they still need guidance on setting their group up for success. It begins with the first meeting. Everyone aims to connect and eventually engage in meaningful conversations. It's going to be in this meeting that you'll set the relational bar, respect quotient, and expectations on how to listen. But if you don't let your group know how to do that and get them to buy in, it's going to be challenging to help direct it to happen. This is why our first meeting starts with a meal and some upbeat interaction questions to start. If your format allows it, having a potluck is a bigger win than most realize. Before anyone shows up, they are already contributors to the group. Instantly it communicates, "You're important and needed here."

The Life Groups Study Questions also look different for that first meeting; they are mixer questions designed to be fun and engaging. No tough questions. What is the shortest distance between two people?—Humor and food. That's what connects people. It helps it go well. After all the fun, we then ask, "What are you looking forward to in the group, and why did you join?" It is a fantastic question. We ask that at the beginning of every quarter, and we often get the same answers, and that's okay. It's going to get me into the Word more often. It's going to keep us connected with the group more often. It gives me a place to process life and what God is talking to me about more often. This is a great setup for the leader to set the vision on how to have great group times together and ensure it's a safe place to be engaged, heard, and cared for.

The leader typically follows up with something like this: "These are great things everyone shared. For us to be able to do what you're talking about, here's how we can allow that to happen and keep on track each week. This is where we start with the four S's—*Share, Study, Support, Serve*. We're here to share about life and what's going on. We're here to study God's Word and see how it applies to our lives. We're here to support each other when there are needs that come up that you share. And we're here to continue to live our faith out by serving those around us in day-to-day life.

Notice, it's not just study. It's not just to discuss the curriculum. It's all of those. We ask our leaders to have the group confirm that these are values to them as well."

Next, we have our leaders address the marks of a healthy group.

Five Marks of a Healthy Group:

1) *Spiritual growth and health* are our number one priority. There may be tangents in our conversations, and that's okay at times. However, I will need to bring us back on track. By stating this at the beginning, the leader gives themselves permission to guide the conversation.

2) *We're here to accept one another.* We all have different preferences, different music we're into, different styles of parenting, different politics. We aren't here to debate any of these things, especially politics. We also always give this quick reminder: "There aren't going to be any political parties in heaven, only followers of Jesus."

3) *We're here to take care of one another.* When a crisis happens, we're there to help with support, prayer, encouragement, listening, and meals.

4) *We want to treat each other with respect.* This is where we talk to our leaders to really lean in on this point. Our goal is to listen to one another; there's nothing worse than another conversation going on when someone shares. We're here to listen and not give advice unless asked. Be undeniably intolerant of gossip. If you hear it, stop it immediately.

More subtly but just as insidious, be careful of gossip prayers. If it wouldn't sound good to the ears of Jesus, it shouldn't sound good to ours. No put-downs. I can be the king of sarcasm, and I must be so careful of that. And again, what is said in our meeting, we want to keep here in the meeting – of course, we never promise confidentiality if something shared would be harmful to themselves or someone else, and/or if I, as the leader, need to seek counsel on how to respond to an issue.

5) *This is our place to meet, to gather, and to keep our commitments to the group.* If you can't make it, please let us know because we know there's a good reason, so we can pray for you.

Here, we tell the leaders to ask their group again: "Does this sound good? Are you with me on this?" It begins the group with a sense of safety, empowered to engage with each other in a healthy way.

When I came to North Coast 33 years ago, it was the first time I sat in an adult group and saw this model. The mood, direction, and safety I experienced at that very first meeting were unlike any new group I had ever been in. And here we are, still doing it. People want to connect and communicate, but so many don't know how, and they don't realize how much they get in their own way and in the way of others.

This sets your leaders and hosts up on how to lead your group to create respect for one another to be able to listen to. No reasonable person expects you to do whatever they say, but they do expect to be heard. And when people are heard, trust is built. And when trust is built, they're willing to listen, to confide, and even confess. For an example of the leaders guide on covering the Life Group Commitment, visit the Additional Resources Section - Chapter Six.

Staffing - How Many Groups Can One Staff Person Oversee?

This is a question we get asked repeatedly, especially when people hear our take on coaching. The context of the question often comes with the idea that North Coast can do this because of the size of the Life Group staff. There is some truth in that. Ministries, businesses, and organizations prioritize staff for what is most important to them. Ensuring we have enough staff to oversee our group is of high value. Yet, what most don't realize is that the large majority (80%) of our positions are quarter to part-time. We say one full-time pastor and a part-time admin can oversee 100 groups. That would mean if a pastor was overseeing 25 groups, it would only be 25% of their job, assuming they also have some admin support. Having most of our group's team part-time allows us to have many more at the table waking up thinking about groups.

The reason I share this is that oftentimes, churches think it takes more paid staff time than it does. Or, as you've heard me explain throughout these pages, though well-intentioned, we often get caught doing things or creating systems that aren't effective or needed. Having launched eight campuses over the years, we would say in our context, a campus pastor can oversee groups until they get to about 30 groups due to their other responsibilities. That would include about 90 to 120 volunteer leaders and hosts. If creating connection and groups is important to your church, your groups will need quality attention. But maybe not as much as is often thought.

NEXT STEPS STRATEGY: What do we need to need to start, stop, tweak, or keep?

Assess how you have communicated to your leaders about staff's availability to leaders. Are there any changes you need to make?

Training your leaders on how to handle issues is foundational to the amount and kind of help you, as staff, will need to offer your leaders. When trained in simple, clear ways, leaders typically rise to the occasion. Is there any training you need to offer your leaders or staff to increase their competence and confidence in helping others?

What level of training is needed to help your leaders become questions askers instead of advice-givers? How does that training get accomplished practically?

If you are going to increase the focus on your groups ministry, how will it be staffed? Are there any opportunities to reallocate staffing responsibilities, or do you have any volunteer ministry partners that would have time to lend to support the workload?

CHAPTER 7

Observe Someone Monitoring Your Results

"Never mistake activity for achievement. Success is never final; failure is never fatal. It's courage that counts." - John Wooden

"Be sure you know the conditions of your flocks. Give careful attention to your herds." - Proverbs 27:23

I golf, but I'm not a golfer. That means I golf a few times a year and can enjoy it on most days. But chances are most great golfers wouldn't want to join me because I'd slow them down too much. Any regular golfer would also probably know I'm not very good once they see my swing, even without seeing me hit the ball. That's not to say I never hit it well or don't have good days; it just can't be counted on. Yet, most of that doesn't matter to me because that's not why I play golf. I play golf because I'm with a group of friends having a good time. My less-than-stellar skills and poor results don't (usually) stress me out to the extent they ruin my time with friends.

As a pastor, we want to make sure we don't treat our ministries like I treat my golf game. I'll do my best and won't worry about the rest; God's got this. Wait, that sounds biblical. Yes, it does. And it is. There are plenty of Proverbs that tell us to lay our plans before our God and leave success to him (Prov. 16:3; 21:31). They've comforted me time and again and helped me lean on him and his Spirit, not just my strategy. Yet, we have to be careful about letting it become an excuse to not evaluate our strategies, which may be wasting time and resources with little results (Prov. 11:14; 15:22). Being busy doesn't mean we're being effective.

There are many evaluative methods you can use to assess your church as a whole. You'll have to decide, if you haven't yet, how you want to go about doing that. Much of what will drive your group's evaluation will be based on the purpose you have for them and how that fits into your church as a whole.

Here are the three categories we use to observe how we're doing and to help identify what we need to start, stop, or continue doing for the health of our groups.

Categories

1) Develop a simple attendance and reporting process.

By now, you can see how important attendance is to us. It gives us key insights into a group's health (Chapter 1), and poor attendance can be used to identify when a leader needs additional support (Chapter 4). However, those insights can only be gleaned if you're getting accurate, relevant information in a timely manner. So, how does that happen? Let me start by sharing how we used to handle attendance and what we've learned throughout the digital age.

Attendance reporting is something we've always done. In the beginning, we used a paper system, which worked well because of the number of groups we had. Then came the digital age to save us, as most church database systems now provide group attendance options.

We knew that we had to maintain an easy system that could be completed in less than 60 seconds. The day after a group meets, the admin who oversees that group will send an attendance reminder email. This weekly communication is also a great opportunity for our admins to connect with the leaders they help oversee and drop a reminder about an upcoming event, include a minor update, or even give a quick encouragement.

Then, there is a link to that leader's personalized roster, and the leader will checkmark who is present. The most important piece is that we know exactly who was there, not just the total number of attendees.

Finally, we ask for feedback, comments, and updates. This open box allows our leaders to share any information that is relevant to that specific meeting. Here are examples of things we typically see in that comment box:

- *An explanation for why someone was missing* – Jake was on a business trip but will return next week.

- *A specific prayer request* – Susie begins her chemo on Tuesday; pray for her!

- *A story about the evening* – We had our social tonight and loved playing the mini golf course together! Super fun time.

- *Service Project Updates* – We created a plan to bring dinner to the shelter. We look forward to completing our service project in two weeks.

However, we also ask our leaders to use that section to report any major issues occurring within the group. Things we have seen include marital crises, addictions, drug or alcohol abuse, emotional, physical, and sexual abuse, among many others.

Most don't add comments, which is okay with us, but it remains an important way for them to communicate with us. And they do.

So when the team looks at the attendance each week (Mondays are our designated day for attendance reports), the staff is looking for overall attendance trends and how we can respond to comments on their feedback. Our leaders know this is another direct line of communication to our staff. Yes, looking at the trends is important, but this also provides a great inlet to provide pastoral care to our leaders and our congregation.

So, what happens when they don't do the attendance tracking? We follow up with them. After the second reminder, we have the pastor reach out to connect with them to problem-solve. That's how important it is to us.

2) Provide a Way for All Participants to Give You Feedback

As we mentioned earlier, healthy organizations and relationships allow you to provide both positive and negative feedback, which, in turn, you can evaluate. During the last week of the quarter, every participant in the group receives an email with an opportunity for them to give feedback on how the group experience went for that quarter. These feedback forms are never anonymous; we require names. Why? Because without names, we wouldn't have context for the comments made, and we also wouldn't have a way to follow up with pastoral care if something comes to light.

The results are shared with pastors and leaders. Most of the responses serve as affirmations and provide significant encouragement to our leaders. The feedback also helps us identify any trends that warrant closer examination, allowing us to support and further develop our leaders. I recall a time when my group didn't give me, the pastor, top scores on our prayer time. While I wasn't entirely surprised (I was aware we didn't pray much), seeing several scores drop from "4 out of 5" to "3" indicated that it was time for change. This feedback not only suggested we needed to pray more but also that I should allocate more time for connecting on life events rather than merely discussing questions.

As with our weekly attendance, we know the feedback forms have to be quick and simple for our group members to fill out, using a rating system of one to five stars for most of the questions.

Here are the questions we have on our survey.

- How would you rate your Life Group?
- How would you rate your group discussion?
- How would you rate the study questions?
- How would you rate your group prayer time?
- Has your group helped you grow in any of the following areas? *(Weekly encouragement / Read and apply scripture / Personal study of scripture / Process life decisions / Support in life's challenges / other)*
- For the next Life Group quarter, I'm planning on: *(continuing in the same group / trying a new group / taking a break from groups)*
- Do you have any additional comments, questions, or concerns?

3) Track Your Trends

Chapter 2 shared the purpose of tracking the numbers in our key vital signs. Remember, people do not act because of numbers; instead, the numbers represent people and trends. Let's dive into exactly how we get these numbers.

Vital Signs of a Healthy Groups Ministry:

- *Percentage of adult weekend attendance in groups:* Our goal is to have 80% of regular adult yearly weekend attendance in a group. For the past 12 years, we've been at 90% or higher. Here's how we came up with that number. Every year in the same month, we take the average number of adults attending our weekend services and compare it to the total number in our groups. We use week four of the quarter to get our number of people in groups because we know that some people will sign up but never show up. We want the count to represent the actual number of people attending our groups regularly and do not count those who signed up but never showed up or only attended one or two times.

- *Group attendance and retention*: Are people showing up to the group regularly and staying in the group long term? These are both important indicators if the goal is to build significant relationships. People typically go where their friends are. Of course, there are valid reasons to leave a group - they've moved, had a job change, experienced a life change, or wanted to try a new group, etc. But if the majority are repeatedly leaving one group, or if this is happening in your groups overall, it's time to dig in and find out what the cause is.

    If this is occurring with one group repeatedly, it could be a leadership issue or a strong personality in the group that is causing friction, for example. If this is happening across all your groups, it could be due to the curriculum, the length of commitment, or the size of the group being either too small or too large. There are lots of possibilities, but getting the data alerts you that something is going on.

- *Recruitment and retention of leadership*: Are we keeping or losing our leaders? We believe everything rises and falls on leadership. People want to lead and be successful. If they're not staying, we need to ask if there is something we need to start or stop doing to keep them around. The question is not if you've lost any leaders, as we all do. The question is why you've lost leaders and at what percentage. The national average for volunteers fulfilling their commitment is 65%. Our hope is to be at least 75%. God gives us plenty of leaders to do the task, though they may feel like they're hiding sometimes, right? Again, there are good reasons to leave leadership positions, but losing too many indicates a change is needed.

- *Group Signups*: Are we offering plenty of groups at multiple local locations on multiple days? People need options. Groups meeting on only one night of the week aren't reaching your entire church; they're only reaching the people who have that time available. We project the number of openings needed based on our weekend attendance and our growth in the last year. To ensure we have plenty of options, we also increased our number of required openings by 10% - 15%.

If we completely fill our groups, we know we've failed! Wait… failed? Yes! I imagine that caught you off guard, but it's true. Chapter Five, Connect Someone, also provides some insight into this. But you need to know that not having this 10% - 15% buffer and filling all groups can be a subtle yet significant limiter to the number of people who sign up.

- *Community Service*: Again, I go back to Ephesians 2:10; we're created to do good works in Christ. About 17 years ago, we asked our groups to consider doing some sort of service project. I didn't think very many would, and it wasn't a majority by any means. But it came back, and it was clear that 30% of our groups went out and did a service project on their own.

We were surprised at first. In fact, highly encouraged. What I have found in leadership is that if you put a half-baked idea out there, you usually still can get about 20 to 30% of the group to go out and do it. We knew we did not want our groups to be inward-focused, and we'd seen the power of serving together. Also, at that time, it was the beginning of the TV home makeover era, including the hit show *Extreme Makeover*. People loved to serve, make an impact, and build that connection with their group as they served. And we knew the spirit was moving within our congregation, compelling us to serve. So, as shocked as we were that 30% completed a service project that year, we still asked – why not more? Here are the three reasons why: Our leaders didn't have the time to organize a service project, they didn't know where to serve or what to do, and/or they didn't have the resources to do that.

One year later, we were still committed to making community service part of our groups and truly believed that our people would serve if we set up projects for them. A key thing for us was that we didn't want to create the projects from scratch because there were already plenty of nonprofit organizations that needed help and had established community service projects to participate in. So, we began to partner with those nonprofits in our community, giving our congregation access to the organizations that need help. By working with the partner organizations, 70% of our groups completed service projects. It worked, by working with the experts in the community!

Sixteen years later, we are well-known throughout our community for our service to them! How great it is to be known for our love for our community, and not just for creating traffic congestion on the weekends. We have, on average, throughout the calendar year, three service projects happening a day throughout the year.

Another great thing about this model of partnering with existing local non-profits is that community service easily becomes doable for churches of any size. Also, we weren't working only with Christian nonprofits or ones that only line up with our values. We are working with all organizations trying to make a difference in our community and need help. It is living out loving your neighbor.

Nonprofits are always looking for volunteer help. And don't let their possible hesitation of saying yes to your offer stop you. Initially, we had the same experience, but unfortunately, it wasn't unfounded. We found that groups (including churches) often overpromised and underdelivered. Usually, the first time, it went great. But what followed often faltered, leaving the organization in a bind by not having the help they thought they were going to get. It created more problems than solutions.

We quickly knew we needed to do better. It took us at least three years to break through being lumped into their previous experiences to create a reputation that was trusted and invited to come. By being consistent in what we say we'll do, seventeen years later, the opposite is happening, and we are asked to do far more in the community than we can say yes to simply because we have upheld our word. There is a link to our community service resource webpage in the Additional Resource Section (at the end of the book).

NEXT STEPS STRATEGY: What do we need to need to start, stop, tweak, or keep?

Are any of the tracking observation tools important for you to begin to develop and or improve? Weekly attendance process, tracking trends, group feedback forms?

When it comes to tracking trends, how are you doing? Which one is most important to you?

- *Percentage of adult weekend attendance in groups:*
- *Group attendance and retention:*
- *Recruitment and retention of leadership:*
- *Group Signups:*
- *Community Service:*

Remember, it takes time and strategy to move forward. You decide what you can and can't do in the allotted time and resources you have. You can't do more than that. Strategic timing and purposeful next steps to build are key to this.

CHAPTER 8

Developing a Game Plan

"Change is inevitable, progress is not."
- Max McKeown

The horse is made ready for the day of battle, but
victory rests with the Lord. - Proverbs 21:31

Creating a Pathway for Change

Most have heard that people don't like change, and there's truth in that statement. But to say no one ever likes change is simply not true. If you received a call today and were told you were receiving a $10,000 yearly raise with no additional responsibility in your job, chances are you would welcome the change and celebrate it! However, change becomes quite difficult when you're offered a $10,000 raise with increased responsibilities that cause you to work unreasonable hours without the support you need. Would that $10,000 be worth it, then? The key questions to ask when offering a change to others are: What will we gain, what will we lose, and does the benefit of the gain outweigh the pain of the loss?

Whenever you add something, you are taking away time, energy, or resources from something else. When you take that thing away, someone typically also loses power, prestige, or position. Knowing that, this decision for change must be weighed carefully and with intentionality.

Over the years, I've learned never to bring a new idea to your full team without running it by others first. Start with a select few key influencers to get their thoughts, their ideas, and, most importantly, their pushbacks. Through their discernment, it would be good to gain an understanding of:

- What losses are there going to be?
- What pushbacks can we expect to receive?
- What are the sacred cows you need to pay attention to? These are the things within your church that may seem untouchable.
- What are the ideas you need to keep pursuing?
- And, most importantly, if, when, and how can you begin to implement this change?

The speed of implementation in our culture is highly valued, and with passion and excitement about something new comes a feeling of wanting to rush ahead quickly. Yet, be careful that it doesn't cause you to avoid collaborating with others on these questions. Putting intentionality and discernment into implementing change will be crucial as you work at increasing your ministry's effectiveness and connection with the people in your church and community, to Jesus, and to one another. Leadership is not a solo sport, just as following Jesus is not a solo sport!

Follow this Change Matrix to help you process and ask the necessary questions in order to move forward.

Change Matrix Process Questions:

What will you gain?

- More effective?
- More efficient?
- More productive?

What will be lost (and what will it cost)?

- Power, control, prestige or position?
- Experience or connections?
- Give up to go up—what are you saying no to, to allow the space to do the new thing?

Who are you going to process change with to ensure you are making a good decision and presenting it in a way that is effective? Never bring a new idea cold to a group; process it in smaller settings to be aware of how to best present it, and know what the issues are.

- Who are one or two people you can begin to process with to think through the issues?
- Who are the two or three influencers that need to know?
- When and how do these groups need to hear about it? Who are the early, middle, and late adopters?
- What individuals need to hear about this before you present to a larger group?

Strategy Planning Arrow

Purpose	Strategy					Priorities
	Barrier Breakers To Start, Stop, Tweak or Keep	How to Measure	Action Steps	Point Person	Target Date for Completion	
	Ask					What we have to do in the next six months...
	Equip					
	Connect					
	Support					What we have to do in the next year...
	Observe					

To access the downloadable version of this chart,
see the QR code at the end of the book.

With caution and collaboration in mind, you can now begin to implement this change. In the Additional Resources Section, you will find a Strategy Planning Arrow that you can implement based on what you have gathered from this book. There is also a link to a video to walk you through this process.

The first goal is to create a clear purpose for small groups within your church. That purpose will be your driving factor and provide clarity and encouragement as you go through this process. Once you have that established, you will begin to strategize. For each of the five areas that we have covered— *Ask, Equip, Connect, Support,* and *Observe*—you can list what the barriers are. What are the things you need to start or stop doing? What can you tweak or keep? And how can you measure those? People are not numbers, but numbers represent people, and you must be able to measure effectiveness. Then, list the action steps for each of the five areas and assign a point person. Setting a target date for the completion of these tasks also helps you track and measure progress. Know that change takes strategic timing and is a process.

The last step will be to identify your priorities. What needs to be completed within the next month? The next six months? Where will your groups be in a year? Following the Strategy Planning Arrow is crucial for staying on track during implementation and for providing clarity to your leadership team when communicating the vision for groups.

No matter your church's size, location, or historical context, relationships are the foundation of the gospel—with Jesus and others! It is my hope that these principles and processes can help you and your people connect so that you can create a lifeline of relationships in following Jesus and reaching out to others to do the same. Please know that we are here to help if you would like further coaching and/or resources moving forward.

THANK YOU FOR READING THIS BOOK!

Thanks so much for taking the time to go through this book! Please know that we are here to help you as you work toward building connection in your church. To support you further and say thanks, we would like to give you a few free bonus resources, no strings attached! I encourage you to scan the QR Code to access these free resources.

Scan the QR Code:

I appreciate your interest in my book, and value your feedback as it helps me improve future versions. I would appreciate it if you could leave your honest, authentic review on Amazon.com with your feedback. Thank you!

Want someone to walk through this with you? Visit DaveEnns.com for more information about:

- *One-on-one coaching with Dave*
- *Small Group Leader Tools Webpage*
- *North Coast Life Groups Webpage*
- *New Leader Training Resource*
- *Sermon-Based Starter Kit*
- *And more!*

REFERENCES

https://www.britannica.com/biography/Johannes-Gutenberg

https://ourworldindata.org/literacy

https://heart.bmj.com/content/102/13/1009

https://www.hhs.gov/about/news/2023/05/23/surgeon-general-issues-new-advisory-about-effects-social-media-use-has-youth-mental-health.html

Larry Osborne, Sticky Church (Michigan: Zondervan, 2008), p. 42